Edgar Cayce on
the Akashic Records

Other Books by Kevin J. Todeschi

Edgar Cayce's ESP

The Edgar Cayce Ideal's Workbook

Edgar Cayce on Soul Mates

Edgar Cayce on the Akashic Records

*Edgar Cayce on the Reincarnation of
Biblical Characters*

Edgar Cayce on the Reincarnation of Famous People

The Encyclopedia of Symbolism

*Soul Development: Edgar Cayce's
Approach for a New World*

Twelve Lessons in Personal Spirituality

Edgar Cayce on
the Akashic Records

The Book of Life

KEVIN J. TODESCHI

ARE
PRESS

ASSOCIATION FOR
RESEARCH AND
ENLIGHTENMENT

A.R.E. Press • Virginia Beach • Virginia

Copyright © 1998
by Kevin J. Todeschi

9th Printing, June 2004

Printed in the U.S.A.

A.R.E. Press
215 67th Street
Virginia Beach, VA 23451-2061

Todeschi, Kevin J.
  Edgar Cayce on the Akashic Records, the book of life / Kevin
J. Todeschi.
      p.   cm.
  ISBN 0-87604-401-1
  1. Akashic Records. 2. Cayce, Edgar, 1877-1945. I. Title.
BF1045.A44T63   1998
133.9—dc21   97-42767

Cover design by Lightbourne Images

*To those souls who never really forget whence
they came or whither they were going . . .*

And I saw the dead, small and great, stand before God; and the books were opened: and another book was opened, which is the book of life: and the dead were judged out of those things which were written in the books, according to their works.

Revelation 20:12

Contents

Preface .... *xi*

Part One: The Past

1 The Akashic Records as a Chronicler of the Past 1

2 Case History—The Family of Anna Campbell 17

3 Recognizing Insights from Your Own Past 43

Part Two: The Present

4 The Akashic Records as an Indicator of the
 Present 67

5 Case Histories 90

6 Working with the Present 99

Part Three: The Future

7 The Akashic Records and Probabilities and
 Potentials 121

8 Case Histories 139

9 Discovering Insights into Your Future 157

Conclusion *177*

Preface

———

It is no exaggeration to state that the computer has transformed (and is still transforming) the planet. Whether it's technology, transportation, communication, education, or entertainment, the computer age has revolutionized the globe and the ways that we understand and interact with one another. No segment of modern society has gone unaffected. The amount of information now stored in computer memory and crossing the internet highway daily is literally unfathomable. And yet, this vast complex of computer systems and collective databases cannot begin to come close to the power, the memory, or the omniscient recording capacity of the Akashic Records.

For ease of understanding, the Akashic Records or

"The Book of Life" can be likened to the universe's supercomputer system. "Akasha" comes from a Sanskrit word meaning "boundless space" and is equated to the central storehouse of all information for every individual who has ever lived. More than just a reservoir of events, the Akashic Records contain every deed, word, feeling, thought, and intent that has occurred at any time in the history of the world. Much more than simply a memory storehouse, these Akashic Records are interactive; they have a tremendous influence upon our everyday lives, our relationships, our feelings and belief systems, and the potentials and probabilities we draw toward us.

The Akashic Records contain the history of every soul since the dawn of creation. These records connect each of us to one another. They contain the stimulus for every archetypal symbol or mythic story which has ever deeply touched patterns of human behavior and experience. They have been the inspiration for dreams and invention. They draw us toward or repel us from one another. They mold and shape levels of human consciousness. They are a portion of Divine Mind. They are the unbiased judge and jury that attempt to guide, educate, and transform every individual to become the very best that she or he can be. They embody an ever-changing fluid array of possible futures that are called into potential as we interact and learn from the data that has already been accumulated.

Information about these Akashic Records—this Book of Life—can be found in folklore, in myth, and throughout the Old and New Testaments. It is traceable at least as far back as the Semitic peoples and includes the Arabs, the Assyrians, the Phoenicians, the Babylonians, and the Hebrews. Among each of these peoples was the belief that there is in existence some kind of celestial tablets which contain the history of humankind as well as all manner of spiritual information.

The first reference in Scripture to some nonearthly volume is found in Exodus 32:32. After the Israelites had committed a most grievous sin by worshiping the golden calf, it was Moses who pleaded on their behalf, offering to take full responsibility and have his own name stricken "out of thy book which thou hast written" in recompense for their deed. Later, in the Old Testament, we learn that there is nothing about an individual that is not known in this same book. In Psalm 139, David makes reference to the fact God has written down everything about him and all the details of his life—even that which is imperfect and those deeds which have yet to be performed.

For many individuals this Book of Life is simply a symbol of those destined for heaven and has its roots in the custom of recording genealogical records of names or perhaps early census taking. Traditional religion suggests that this book—either in literal or symbolic form—contains the names of all those who are worthy of salvation. The book is to be opened in connection with divine judgment (Dan. 7:10, Rev. 20:12). In the New Testament, those redeemed by Christ are contained within the book (Philippians 4); those not found in the book of life will not enter the kingdom of heaven.

As an interesting corollary, in the ancient world a person's name was symbolic of that individual's existence. According to Sir James George Frazer, author of *The Golden Bough*—one of the most extensive volumes on world mythology—there was such a bond between one's name and one's existence "that magic may be wrought on a man just as easily as through his name as through his hair, his nails, or any other material part of his person." In ancient Egypt, to blot a person's name out of a record was equivalent to destroying the fact that he or she had ever existed.

Closer to our current era, a great deal of contemporary information on the Akashic Records has been made available by both reputable psychics and modern-day mystics—individuals who have somehow perceived beyond the limits of three dimensions. According to H.P. [Helena Petrovna] Blavatsky (1831-1891), Russian immigrant, mystic, and founder of the Theosophical Society, the Akashic Records are much more than simply an account of static data which may be gleaned by a sensitive. Instead, the records have an ongoing creative stimulus upon the present:

> Akasha is one of the cosmic principles and is a plastic matter, creative in its physical nature, immutable in its higher principles. It is the quintessence of all possible forms of energy, material, psychic, or spiritual; and contains within itself the germs of universal creation, which sprout forth under the impulse of the Divine Spirit.
>
> *Alchemy and the Secret Doctrine*

Rudolf Steiner (1861-1925), the Austrian-born philosopher, educator, and founder of the Anthroposophical Society, possessed the ability to perceive information beyond the material world: a "spiritual world" which was just as real to him as the physical world was to others. Steiner claimed that the ability to perceive this other world could be developed, enabling an individual to see events and information every bit as concrete as the present:

> . . . man can penetrate to the eternal origins of the things which vanish with time. A man broadens his power of cognition in this way if he is no longer limited to external evidence where knowledge of the past is concerned. Then he can *see* in events

what is not perceptible to the senses, that part which time cannot destroy. He penetrates from transitory to non-transitory history. It is a fact that this history is written in other characters than is ordinary history. In gnosis and in theosophy it is called the "Akasha Chronicle" ... To the uninitiated, who cannot yet convince himself of the reality of a separate spiritual world through his own experience, the initiate easily appears to be a visionary, if not something worse. The one who has acquired the ability to perceive in the spiritual world comes to know past events in their eternal character. They do not stand before him like the dead testimony of history, but appear in full *life*. In a certain sense, what has happened takes place before him.

Cosmic Memory

In terms of contemporary insights, perhaps the most extensive source of information regarding the Akashic Records comes from the clairvoyant work of Edgar Cayce (1877-1945), Christian mystic and founder of the Association for Research and Enlightenment, Inc. For forty-three years of his adult life, Edgar Cayce possessed the ability to lie down on a couch, close his eyes, fold his hands over his stomach, and put himself into some kind of an altered state in which virtually any type of information was available. The accuracy of Cayce's psychic work is evidenced by approximately one dozen biographies and literally hundreds of books and tapes which explore various aspects of his information and the thousands of topics he discussed.

When asked about the source of his information, Cayce replied that there were essentially two. The first was the subconscious mind of the individual for whom he was giving the reading and the second was the

Akashic Records. In further describing these records, Cayce stated:

> Upon time and space is written the thoughts, the deeds, the activities of an entity—as in relationships to its environs, its hereditary influence; as directed—or judgment drawn by or according to what the entity's ideal is.
>
> Hence, as it has been oft called, the record is God's book of remembrance; and each entity, each soul—as the activities of a single day of an entity in the material world—either makes same good or bad or indifferent, depending upon the entity's application of self towards that which is the ideal manner for the use of time, opportunity and the EXPRESSION of that for which each soul enters a material manifestation.
>
> The interpretation then as drawn here is with the desire and hope that, in opening this for the entity, the experience may be one of helpfulness and hopefulness.
>
> 1650-1*

Most often, when giving a reading which discussed a person's soul history and the individual's sojourn through space and time, Cayce would begin with a statement such as "Yes, we have before us the records of the entity now known or called _____." In describing the process for accessing these records, Edgar Cayce stated:

---

*The readings were all numbered to provide confidentiality. The first set of numbers (e.g., "1650") refers to the person or group for whom the reading was given. The second set of numbers (e.g., "1") refers to the number in the series. In this example (1650-1), the number represents the first reading for the individual assigned [1650].

I see myself as a tiny dot out of my physical body, which lies inert before me. I find myself oppressed by darkness and there is a feeling of terrific loneliness. Suddenly, I am conscious of a white beam of light. As this tiny dot, I move upward following the light, knowing that I must follow it or be lost.

As I move along this path of light I gradually become conscious of various levels upon which there is movement. Upon the first levels there are vague, horrible shapes, grotesque forms such as one sees in nightmares. Passing on, there begin to appear on either side misshapen forms of human beings with some part of the body magnified. Again there is change and I become conscious of gray-hooded forms moving downward. Gradually, these become lighter in color. Then the direction changes and these forms move upward and the color of the robes grows rapidly lighter. Next, there begin to appear on either side vague outlines of houses, walls, trees, etc., but everything is motionless.

As I pass on, there is more light and movement in what appear to be normal cities and towns. With the growth of movement I become conscious of sounds, at first indistinct rumblings, then music, laughter, and singing of birds. There is more and more light, the colors become very beautiful, and there is the sound of wonderful music. The houses are left behind, ahead there is only a blending of sound and color. Quite suddenly I come upon a hall of records. It is a hall without walls, without ceiling, but I am conscious of seeing an old man who hands me a large book, a record of the individual for whom I seek information.

Case 294-19 Report File

e given the record, Cayce had the ability to select the information which would be most capable of assisting the individual at that time in his or her life. Frequently, a reading might suggest that only a selection of the available material was being provided, but that the individual was being given that which would be "most helpful and hopeful." Additional insights were frequently provided in subsequent readings once an individual had attempted to work with and apply the information which had been given previously.

As a means of perhaps alluding to the fact that the Akashic Records were not simply a transcription of the past but included the present, the future, and certain probabilities as well, in reading 304-5, Cayce began the reading with the curious statement:

> Yes, we have the body here, and the record as has been made and as may be made with the will as exercised, and the condition irrespective of the will's influence or effect as has been created. **We have conditions that might have been, that are and that may be. Do not get the three mixed [up] or crossed purposes of either.** [Author's emphasis]

When discussing the Book of Life, Cayce stated that it was "the record of God, of thee, thy soul within and the knowledge of same" (281-33). In another reading (2533-8), Cayce was asked to explain the difference between the Book of Life and the Akashic Records:

> Q. [What is meant by] The Book of Life?
> A. The record that the individual entity itself writes upon the skein of time and space, through patience—and is opened when self has attuned to

the infinite, and may be read by those attuning to that consciousness . . .

Q. The Book of God's Remembrances?

A. This is the Book of Life.

Q. The Akashic Records?

A. Those made by the individual, as just indicated.

The Edgar Cayce readings suggest that each of us writes the story of our lives through our thoughts, our deeds, and our interactions with the rest of creation. This information has an effect upon us in the here and now. In fact, the Akashic Records have such an impact upon our lives and the potentials and probabilities we draw toward us that any exploration of them cannot help but provide us with insights into the nature of ourselves and our relationship to the universe.

There is much more to our lives, our histories, and our individual influence upon our tomorrows than we have perhaps dared to imagine. By accessing information from the Akashic Records, the universe's computer database, much might be revealed to us. The world as we have collectively perceived it is but a faint shadow of reality. This book has been compiled in the hopes of giving individuals a glimpse beyond that shadow.

Kevin J. Todeschi
Virginia Beach, Virginia

Part One:

The Past

~

Again the specter raised a cry, and shook his chain and
   wrung his shadowy hands.
"You are fettered," said Scrooge trembling. "Tell me
   why?"
"I wear the chain I forged in life," replied the Ghost. "I
   made it link by link, and yard by yard; I girded it on
   of my own free will, and of my own free will I wore
   it . . . "

Conversation between Ebenezer Scrooge
and the ghost of Jacob Marley
Charles Dickens's *A Christmas Carol*

1

The Akashic Records as a Chronicler of the Past

———◆———

The records that have been written have been written...
Then the natural question of the entity, from that which has been given, is: From what source, or how, is such a record read of the activities in the past? How may self know that there is being given a TRUE record of the activities in a period of which there is no written WORD [of] history? Yet the entity itself sees, and is being taught, and is studying, the records that are written in nature, in the rocks, in the hills, in the trees, in that termed the genealogical log of nature itself. Just as true, then, is the record that the mind makes upon the film of time and space in the activities of a body with its soul that is made in the image of the Maker; being then spirit, in its form, upon the records IN time and space.

487-17

*I*magine having a computer system that keeps track of every event, thought, image, or desire that had ever transpired in the earth. Imagine, as well, that rather than simply a compilation of written data and words, this system contains countless videotape film and pictures, providing the viewer with an eyewitness account of all that had ever happened within any historical time frame. Finally, imagine that this enormous database not only keeps track of the information from an objective perspective but also maintains the perspectives and emotions of every individual involved. As incredible as it may sound, this description gives a fairly accurate representation of the Akashic Records.

Edgar Cayce, who has been called the most documented psychic of all time as well as a twentieth-century mystic, helped thousands of people through the use of his remarkable intuitive ability. For over forty years, Cayce gave readings, or psychic dissertations, using the Akashic Records as his primary resource material. Cayce's essential talent was his ability to access and describe information from these records, information which would enable people to discover everything from their essential purpose in life to the underlying cause of a long-standing problem. It was a resource of information, Cayce claimed, which was and is available to everyone.

In an effort to describe how this is feasible, Edgar Cayce stated that it is possible for individuals to attune to the Akashic Records in the same manner that a radio could be built to tune in to radio waves. Although the records are not physical in nature, an individual in attunement can "hear," "read," and "experience" the information nonetheless. In order to illustrate what an individual might perceive while viewing this information, Cayce told an eighteen-year-old girl that the Akashic Records of the mental world might be compared to a movie theater of the physical world (275-19). This movie could be replayed in an effort to understand what had occurred in an individual's experience in any period, at any time, or while in any place in history. Also within this data was a record of lessons learned, opportunities lost, faults acquired, and experiences gained. In addition, although an individual's actions could be misinterpreted or misconstrued in the physical world, the Akashic Records maintained an objective record of a person's "real life" because it reported his or her true intent.

In 1934, while giving a reading to a twenty-eight-year-old freight agent (416-2), Edgar Cayce tried to define these records further. Not only did he discuss what the Akashic Records are, but he explained how they are written, and clarified how an individual could gain access to the information. Apparently, any type of endeavor— whether action, thought, desire, or deed—creates some kind of vibration. This vibration produces a mark upon (what Cayce called) the skein of space and time and is somehow permanently identified with the individual responsible. Although unseen, it is an etheric energy that is as evident to a sensitive as the printed word is to a sighted person:

> When there is the thought or the activity of the body in any particular environ, this very activity makes for the impressions upon the soul . . .
>
> As to the records made by such an activity, these are written upon what is known as time or space; much in the form or manner as are the messages that are of a familiar nature to the body in its present activity. As the instruments of recording are used, so does the activity of ENERGY expended leave its imprint upon the etheric wave that records between time and space that DESIRED to be put, as to that impelling or producing. Just as the figures or characters make for communications between in-

dividuals, so does the soul upon the pages or records of time and space.

416-2

Complicating our ability to understand and work with these records, however, Cayce explained to his wife, Gertrude, in reading 538-32 that it is very possible for anyone attempting to read the records (a psychic, a sensitive individual, the entity itself, etc.) to misinterpret the information. Perceiving the Akashic database is apparently shaded by the mental experience and background of the person reading the information UNLESS the intent is totally selfless and desirous of being of help. In other words, two individuals could acquire very different interpretations from the very same records because of their own belief systems, backgrounds, experiences, and personal motives.

During the course of a reading given to a thirty-eight-year-old physician, the subjective nature of the Akashic Records was explained as follows:

> Hence the interpretations of these may vary somewhat, dependent upon what phases the approach is made. In the same manner that in material experiences entities, viewing an event or happening, are prompted to give THEIR version according to the reaction upon their ideal—and upon those promptings of the purpose of the individual so viewing same.

1448-2

The same person was told that every experience encountered in an individual's life could leave a good or a bad impression upon these Akashic Records. Apparently each occurrence in life has the capacity to be a constructive or a destructive influence, based upon what an individual does with that experience. Different choices will leave very different impressions upon the records.

Since these records are so complete, so accurate, and so individualized, a logical question might be: *Just what is the purpose of the Akashic Records in the first place?* Simply put, the answer is to keep track of and assist with each soul's personal growth and transformation. However, in order to adequately discuss and understand Edgar Cayce's perception of the records, one needs to possess an adequate background in what might be termed "the Cayce Cosmology." Essentially, that cosmology can be summed up in the statement: *God is essentially love and the Universe is completely orderly.* Beyond that concept is the premise that each individual was purposefully created, as a soul, to become a companion with the Creator.

Confirming Scripture, according to the Cayce readings, we were created in "God's image" (Genesis 1:26) and therefore our natural state is spirit. Life did not begin at the moment of physical birth, rather there was an existence in spirit prior to physicality. God gave to each soul complete freedom of choice and the opportunity to find expression—to find themselves, so to speak. Because souls are created in God's image, it would only be through a process of personal experiences—one choice leading to another, and then another, and then another—that God's companions could gain their own individuality, truly being a part of Him and yet individuals in their own right. Once they have discovered their individuality they would once again return in consciousness to be His companions and cocreators.

From Cayce's perspective, although we are currently having a physical experience, our bodies are simply a temporal home. Just as an automobile is discarded when the owner no longer finds it useful, so too are our bodies set aside when they have completed their function. We are not physical bodies with souls, but are spiritual beings who happen to be having a physical existence. If this is true and we are fundamentally spiritual beings, then we might ask: *So, just what are we doing here?* The answer proposed by the Cayce information is that **we are essentially gathering experiences.**

According to the readings, the soul, basically creative in nature, longs to find self-expression. In fact, the essential question repeatedly posed by the soul might be: *Who am I?* This question is addressed in infinite ways as each soul chooses specific experiences to meet itself. The soul gains firsthand knowledge not only about its own identity but also learns how choices lead to certain experiences. In time, soul experiences and acquired knowledge will lead to wisdom. Inevitably, wisdom will lead to compassion and eventually love will be the end result. At this point, the soul will know its individual identity as well as its true relationship with God. The soul will have come to understand that its primary essence and God's are one and the same, *LOVE:*

> Thus innately the entity is ever desiring to try something new. This is well, provided the basis of such is builded upon truth. For truth in any clime is ever the same—it is law. And love is law, law is love. Love is God, God is Love. It is the universal consciousness, the desire for harmonious expressions for the good of all, that is the heritage in man, if there is the acceptance of the way and manner such may be applied, first in the spiritual purpose and then in the mental application, and the material success will be pleasing to any.
>
>   3350-1

The soul's education in self-awareness is undertaken through a process of cause and effect. This cause-and-effect growth pattern was examined in nearly two thousand Cayce readings which explored the topic of reincarnation. Rather than being a fatalistic process, the influence from one's past merely provides a framework of potentials and probabilities. These possibilities are all inscribed upon the Akashic Records. An individual's choices, actions, and free will in the present actually determine the experience lived this time around. For Cayce, it wasn't nearly so important as to who an individual had once been (or even what he or she had been doing), as it was paramount that the individual focus on the present and the opportunities and the challenges that faced the person in this time, in this place, right now. In the language of the readings:

> In the studies, then, know WHERE ye are going
> . . . to find that ye only lived, died and were buried
> under the cherry tree in Grandmother's garden
> does not make thee one whit [a] better neighbor,
> citizen, mother or father!
> But to know that ye spoke unkindly and suffered
> for it, and in the present may correct it by being
> righteous—THAT is worth while!
>
> 5753-2

One young woman was told that from the past she had an innate gift for music (275-33), and that through meditation and attunement she could reawaken those talents in the present: "For, as an individual attunes itself to that which it has attained, even at a MOMENT of time, there is aroused the abilities to KNOW even that which WAS known through the [past] experience." In another instance, a forty-six-year-old woman who received a reading about her past lives was told which lifetimes were having the greatest effect upon the present (757-8). Her reading detailed incarnations in Colonial America, England during the Crusades, ancient Persia, and ancient Egypt. From each of these experiences, certain inclinations had been developed and still remained a part of the woman's personality and individuality. In America, she had acquired the ability to assist individuals in cooperating and communicating with one another so that people of various backgrounds and motives could learn to work together. From long periods of isolation in England, she retained an inner longing to always make time in her life for personal reflection and contemplation. From an incarnation as Persian nobility, she had acquired the desire to be surrounded by finery and beauty. Her interest in religious thought was traced to a similar work she had begun in ancient Egypt. Each of these traits simply acted as influences in the woman's current life. Nothing was fixed; instead, the woman could use, abuse, or even ignore these inclinations in her life right now.

For example, the woman's impulse to be alone could be used in the present as times for personal rejuvenation in order to better assist those around her; however, it might just as easily be directed into a sense of aloofness or the selfish desire to always put her own needs first. In Cayce's understanding, influences from the past are always molded and shaped by an individual's will, desires, and purposes in the present.

In addition to the past-life material, interesting insights presented themselves in this woman's case. During the course of the reading, Cayce described what manner of information was written upon the Akashic Records, how that information made its impression, as well as the influence this type of material could have upon an individual in the present. After putting himself into the trance state and journeying in consciousness to the Akashic Records, Cayce began his discourse. The woman's reading states in part:

> Yes, we have the entity and those relations with the universe and universal forces, that are latent and manifested in the personalities of the entity now known as—or called—[757], as recorded by the experiences in the soul's activity and journey through the environs that make for those impressions—or those that become manifested influences or forces in the experience of an entity in its present sojourn in the earth.
>
> Questions naturally arise in this particular experience of this entity as to how or in what manner the records are made of an entity's sojourn or activity in a sphere or space, so that there are the abilities of one to read or interpret same. Are they as letters written? Are they as pictures of the experiences of an entity? Are they in forms as of omens or characters that represent certain influences or activities about the earth? Yea, all of these, my friend, and more; for they are as but the skein of life itself, the expression of a divine force from the God-Father itself, making manifestations in forms that become manifestations in a material experience. For truly to be absent from the body is to be present with those infinite influences and forces that may act upon and be acted upon, from the emanations of divine influences that may be either visions as picturized, written as thought in characterizations from the various influences through which such entities make for the communication—whether in ideas or in characters that represent those ideas in their expressions as one to another. As in all forms

of communicative influences from one entity or soul to another—in a look, in an expression of some portion of the anatomical influences or form, or from word, or from the turn as from the cut or form of eye, shape or form of mouth, the rising of the brow, or in any communicative influences—these either bespeak of those things that are for the aggrandizement of self's own motives or impulses, or are the expressions of that purpose, that desire, whereunto such a soul or expression or entity has been called. These are forms or manners through which such are written, as in the Book of Life; and may be read and known of men.

757-8

In essence, life is an adventure of experiences whereby an individual is challenged to become a better person for having had those experiences. An experience alone doesn't determine who the individual is as a person, rather it is how the individual chooses to face those experiences. From the perspective of reincarnation, an individual's growth is predicated primarily upon how well he or she deals with the opportunities and circumstances that present themselves in daily life.

Unfortunately, rather than seeing that individuals are very much active "cocreators" in the unfoldment of their life journeys, too often reincarnation has been misinterpreted as a fatalistic journey through experiences and relationships that belong to an individual because of her or his "karma." With this approach, choices made in the past have somehow etched in stone the future, and life is simply a process of going through the motions. This is definitely not the Cayce approach to reincarnation and karma in which each lifetime is one of nearly limitless opportunities. At one point, Edgar Cayce stated that approaches to reincarnation that do not take into account the importance of free will, created what he called a karmic "bugaboo" (136-18)—a total misunderstanding of the laws at work. From his perspective, individuals are very much active participants in their life journeys and not simply sometime-reluctant observers.

The word *karma* is a Sanskrit term that means *work, deed,* or *act.* It can also be interpreted to mean "cause and effect." Although agreeing with this concept, the Edgar Cayce readings make perhaps one of the most intriguing and unique philosophical contributions: the idea that karma can be defined as memory. It is not really a debt that must be paid, nor is it necessarily a set of specific circumstances that must be experienced because of deeds or misdeeds from the past. **Karma is simply patterns of memory.** It is a pool of information stored in the Akashic Records that the subconscious draws upon in the present. It has elements that are positive as well as those which seem negative. For example, an immediate affability toward an individual just met is as likely to be "karmic" as is an immediate animosity toward someone else. To be sure, this subconscious memory has an effect and an influence upon how we think, how we react, what we choose, even how we look! But the component of free will is ever within our grasp.

In one respect, this idea of "karma as memory" can be broken down even further so that we possess memory in terms of desires that we've brought with us from the past, memory in terms of situations that may still need to be learned, and even memory in terms of patterns that we keep choosing to experience, but in simplest terms it can be understood as memory. Although the memory is there, freedom of choice allows an individual to determine the path he or she takes in this present life. In practical terms, we may not always be able to understand why a certain situation was drawn to us, and in fact the *why* may not be of primary importance; what is important is how we choose to respond.

In 1944, while giving a reading to a forty-year-old fireman, Cayce discussed the fact that the past-life information he was drawing upon was specifically related to the life cycle that the individual presently faced. The suggestion given by Gertrude Cayce for accessing the information from the Akashic Records and a portion of the reading follows:

Gertrude Cayce: You will give the relations of this entity and the universe, and the universal forces; giving the conditions which are as personalities, latent and exhibited in the present life; also the former appearances in the earth plane, giving time, place and the name, and that in each life which built or retarded the development for the entity; giving the abilities of the present entity, that to which it may attain, and how. You will answer the questions, as I ask them:

Edgar Cayce: Yes, we have the records here of that entity now known as or called [3902].

In giving the interpretations of the records, written or imposed or impressed upon the skein of time and space, or the Akashic records in God's book of remembrances, these we find:

We would choose from these records that which if applied in the experience will bring a better interpretation of the how and why that there are certain latent and manifested urges in the abilities of the entity in the present, which if applied in a constructive, creative way may bring a better ability of the entity to apply itself in being a channel, a manifestation of those divine influences that are the cause and purpose of the entity's appearance in the earth in the present . . .

As to the appearances in the earth, we find that these have been quite varied. **Not all may be given by any means but these that are a part of the awareness or consciousness of the entity in the present cycle of its experience. And these are at that period that they may be applied.** As indicated the mental is to be applied for the development of the material as well as the mental and spiritual self. Keep self from condemnation ever. [Author's emphasis]

3902-2

Regardless of which cycle has surfaced in one's life, the soul constantly experiences the consequences of its previous choices. This concept is expressed in biblical terminology as "What you sow you must reap" and is generally labeled as "Like attracts like" by students of reincarnation. This essentially means that individuals get to experience for themselves the effects that their previous choices have had upon others. Rather than being predestined, individuals continue to be in control of their lives (and their perceptions) **through how they choose to respond** to the situations they've drawn to themselves. Ultimately all experiences are for one's personal growth.

It is worth noting that soul growth can occur even when an individual has made the "wrong" choice. For example, in one case which will be explored in greater depth in the next chapter, one woman (1523) had obviously made the wrong choice when she married her first husband. However, that choice enabled her and her husband both to overcome certain patterns that had originated two hundred years earlier. Although the memory (or the karma) from the past had to be dealt with, it might have been overcome in an easier fashion. It is interesting to note that the readings often suggested it was better to make an erroneous choice than it was to be idle and to do nothing, because soul development was only possible through movement, growth, and activity.

In Cayce's cosmology, each soul's wealth of experiences from the past acts as subconscious memory in the present. By coming to terms with that memory—which manifests through such things as one's desires, feelings, attributes, even fears—faults and shortcomings can be overcome and talents and abilities expressed.

In terms of personal relationships, Edgar Cayce stated that we never meet anyone by chance, nor do we ever have an emotional connection (positive or negative) to another individual for the very first time. Relationships are an ongoing learning and experiential process. In other words, we pick up our relationship with another person exactly where it was left the last time around. As one example, two individuals from the Cayce files (cases 288 and 294) were told that "These two have ever been together," (294-9) and have experienced every imaginable relationship from father and daughter, employee and employer, mother and son, to husband and wife. In another instance (1222-1), a woman was told that part of the reason her husband was so controlling and demanding was because he had purchased her in a previous life. Cayce stated, "He bought you! Doesn't he act like it at times?" to which the woman responded, "He sure does!" The nature and ongoing development of all relationships are a portion of that which is recorded by the Akashic Records.

An interesting twist on the idea that individuals are constantly meeting the memory they have previously built in relationships with one another is that there really isn't karma *between* people; instead, there is only karma with one's own self. These patterns of behavior and memory are stored within one's own records. The conceptual challenge, however, is that individuals seem to most effectively come to terms with their own karmic memory, or "meet themselves," through their interactions with others. It is this interesting dynamic of meeting oneself through relationships with others that often causes individuals to perceive "them" as the basis of one's frustrations and challenges rather than accepting personal responsibility.

And yet, in spite of the fact that karma belongs to oneself, each soul is constantly drawn toward certain individuals and groups that will enable them to meet themselves in circumstances and relationships. Those individuals and groups, in turn, are drawn toward specific people in an effort to come to terms with their own karmic memory.

This concept of cyclic patterns with groups of individuals is evidenced among Cayce's contemporaries. A number of people who had readings were frequently given lifetimes in history that progressed along the following lines: Atlantis, ancient Egypt, Persia, Palestine, Europe, Colonial America, and then as a contemporary of Cayce's in the first half of the twentieth century. Because of this pattern, and the number of individuals who requested past-life readings for themselves and their families, some individual relationships can be traced for thousands of years.

In an effort to understand the dynamics of group karma that may be at play in our own lives, it's possible to gather insights from the experiences of others. The experiences of these people and the development of their relationships through time can provide us with some interesting insights into how this process of coming to terms with the Akashic Records of the past works, as well as the interconnected dynamic between free choice and karmic memory. By exploring the biographical stories of others against their soul histories, we might discover karma-in-action. The process of life and death, rebirth, and the movement toward individuality is similar for each of us. Looking at the records and the soul histories of others might enable us to make more educated choices for ourselves as we come to terms with our own karmic memory and the meeting of patterns from the past.

With that in mind, one of the most fascinating case histories in the Cayce files is that of a twenty-nine-year-old woman who received her first reading in January 1938. What distinguishes this case from hundreds of others is that over the next six and a half years (before Cayce's death in 1945) this woman procured an astonishing eighty-three readings for seventeen family members. These readings enabled her to understand how some of her current problems related not only to the present, but to a period that had occurred more than one hundred years previously—before she had even been born! More than that, she discovered how a majority of her family grouping had been "entangled" for thousands of years. These events and experiences continued to be written on the Akashic Records, giving impulse and reason to many of the woman's current experiences.

2

Case History—
The Family of Anna Campbell

(Note: The names of case 1523 and her family members have been changed in order to maintain confidentiality.)

In 1938 a twenty-nine-year-old woman came to Edgar Cayce for a psychic reading (case 1523). She was desperate and felt he was her last hope. She was near an end, both physically and mentally. Her marriage was not a happy one, but she was lost as to what to do. She was torn between divorcing her second husband or staying with him. Although unhappy in the situation, part of her hoped to make the marriage work in order to fulfill her dream of having a family.

Her reason for coming to see Mr. Cayce, however, was not for marital advice but because of a physical condition. She was fearful that her situation might require surgery and render her incapable of conception. A tubal pregnancy during her disastrous first marriage had resulted in the removal of one set of fallopian tubes. She had begun to experience similar physical symptoms and feared that a second tubal pregnancy would end her chances of having a baby. More than anything else, she wanted to be a mother. Other family members had pursued college and careers; her sister was working on a master's degree. But not Anna; for as long as she could remember, she had one dream: "to have six children and to grow old with them." She hoped by having a physical reading that she would avoid another operation.

Anna's life history was unknown to Edgar Cayce at the time of her reading. However, an overview of her story will enable us to better understand her situation as well as its connection to the past.

She was born in a very small town at the turn of the twentieth century. So small, in fact, that half a century later the town would have been annexed by surrounding communities and literally disappeared. Her parents were farmers, though her mother had come from a Kentucky background much more refined and dignified than her father's. This fact seemed to bother her father for much of his life. Her father was one of the last frontiersmen, deeply rooted in the land and the knowledge of what it could provide for his family.

She was one of six children who would grow to adulthood and for the most part she got along with all of her siblings with the exception of her older sister. For as long as she could remember, there was antagonism, jealousy, and distrust between the two. Although her parents ran a fairly structured environment—there were chores and studies to be done—her mother had become so frustrated by the years of fighting between Anna and her sister, Vera, that she no longer tried to intercede. It was left for Anna and Vera to fight it out, and fight it out they did.

Although family squabbles are common, the antagonism between the two seemed intensely focused. Interestingly enough, Anna noticed that there appeared to be two others in the household who had as great a difficulty getting along as she and her sister. Her father and her third brother, Warren (born right after Anna), constantly quarreled. It seemed that Warren was always being "switched" for things that one of the other children just might have gotten away with—her father appeared intent on keeping him "in line." For this reason, she felt it was her duty (and her mother's as well) to come to Warren's rescue whenever he was having "the tar whipped out of him" by her dad.

Her mother seemed to get along well with everyone. The woman had even been described as "an angel." Though she and Anna had differing opinions about many things, they were very close. In spite of her mother's kindness, gentility, and compassion, however, one thing seemed completely out of the woman's character: the woman had an intense hatred of Catholics. Her mother had even been known to say that she would rather see one of her children dead than married to a Catholic. The opportunity to change her mind would present itself through one of her sons.

In this rural setting there was always something to occupy Anna's time. Whether it was weeding, cleaning, picking, washing, planting, sewing, ironing, or schooling, free time was minimal. Anna constantly felt that she never got to do what she wanted for there just wasn't time. Families had to work hard just to make a living from the land. Her father built houses on the side and had a few rental properties to make ends meet.

Complicating her young life, Anna found it impossible to escape Vera's presence; the two shared a room. On those few occasions when the lack of chores allowed young friends or cousins to call, Vera tried to sway the visitors to another room with wondrous tales of exciting games they could play—"but not with Anna." As time passed, the elder sister became paranoid whenever male callers came to visit her. She showed an extreme fear that they might give Anna the least bit of attention. She was even jealous of the way Anna looked and acted—though Anna always believed it was her sister who was the model and not herself. Throughout the entire time they grew up together, Vera believed that Anna had gotten "all the breaks" and she none. From Anna's perspective, she didn't feel as though she had gotten any advantages.

In spite of her sister's presence, Anna was relatively happy as a youngster as long as she was home. She had four brothers, two older (Mitchell and Carl) and two younger (Warren and Everett) to keep her company, a father to tag along with whenever she could escape from dishes and household chores, and beautiful dreams of her grownup life as a mother that filled her mind. Her happiness faded and what bliss she had ended, however, as soon as she entered school.

It didn't take her long to realize that other girls didn't like her. They thought of her as a tomboy or a flirt, though neither description was totally accurate. Although their attitude hurt at first, she decided it was fine because she didn't like them much either. She felt much more comfortable around boys, like her brothers, but it wasn't proper to play with boys—even speak to them at some schools. So she became a loner.

Although it might have seemed unusual for a girl in the 1910s, she began in time to excel at two things she could do on her own: music and basketball. As time passed, she stayed a loner, keeping most of her thoughts to herself and wishing for the day when she would have a husband and a family. Eventually she entered the eighth grade when her life would change forever. Although still very much a loner, she became a member of the girl's basketball team. Much of the time, however, she continued to dream wistfully of someone who quite probably didn't exist, someone with whom she could spend the rest of her life.

One day it happened. Seemingly out of nowhere she spotted him. His name was Robert. Although he was several years older than she (and certainly not aware of her existence), she knew he was THE ONE. Anna wasn't quite clear how she knew it, but there was never any doubt that Robert was to be her husband.

This "knowing" was one of several unusual experiences which would shape her life. In one of the first, she had been at her aunt's house in the city. A place she had frequented dozens of times before. Through the back window she could see the marshlands, and the grasses, and the trees off in the distance. Instead of being peaceful, the image suddenly grew more foreboding and frightening as if the fear had been buried deep within her all the time. She began to feel chilled, alone, and more terrified than she had ever been before. Suddenly, she heard herself whisper, "I've got to get out of this place . . . I've got to get out of this place!" The fear subsided just as quickly as it had come, and all that remained was the scene through the back window. She was in her aunt's house, safe and sound, though the happening would remain with her and be called to mind more than twenty years later in the home of Edgar Cayce as he witnessed a similar scene contained in the Akashic Records.

The experience with Robert was similar. She found herself in the schoolyard where dozens of children were playing and laughing and arguing. Suddenly, she happened to look up from what she had been doing in the direction of a group of students not too far away. Instantly, in the midst of all the noise, the excitement of play, and the bouncing of balls, she spotted him, and what happened next would amaze her for the rest of her life:

All at once, the noises began to subside. All the children in the schoolyard began to vanish from her sight and she was completely alone with a boy she didn't even know. There was no sound; there was no one else around. The two of them were all that existed. Her astonishment at the scene caused her to catch her breath, and in the next instant the schoolyard and all its children returned. From that day forth, her dream of a husband would have the face of Robert . . . but it would seem a very long while before he even knew that she was alive.

Finally, toward the first of the year, Anna began to feel more comfortable around some of the children at school. Unfortunately for her reputation, however, all of them were boys. Harsh and untruthful talk among some of the girls continued, and an event toward the end of the eighth grade would ruin her reputation.

One night, when her parents thought she was at a neighborhood party, she and some friends went for an innocent adventure in a car. Her friends, all boys, had "their girls" with them, and Anna was simply along for the ride, dreaming of Robert. The journey started well enough, but instead of soon returning as had been planned, the car broke down miles from home. All of the other girls and most of the boys managed to get rides to their respective houses. Only three of them were left alone—the three who lived near one another—Anna and two of the boys. Hours passed before the three got another car and the boys were able to take Anna home.

Her father had gone to the party looking for her. There he heard wild tales of Anna heading off in a car with "a bunch of boys." The ensuing hours had given him plenty of time to contemplate his worst fears. By the time the trio pulled into the dirt driveway he was waiting for them, rifle in hand.

Without waiting for an explanation, he threatened to kill the boys if they ever laid hands on Anna again. His daughter tried desperately to relate what had happened, but the man was enraged and could not hear a word she was saying. Fearing for their lives, the two boys bolted from the home, and Anna was "whooped" and sent off to bed. Unluckily for Anna, by the next morning the story had spread like wildfire throughout the small town. But it wasn't the story of the car breaking down, or the old man with the gun, or the three and their innocent adventure. Instead it was the story of the young girl and imaginative tales of what she had done late at night with two boys.

Within a week Anna couldn't venture anywhere without having someone point at her and whisper behind their hand about the incident. Her reputation had long been in question, but there no longer remained any doubt. She was branded a loose woman. The episode made her withdraw even more into a place where her only fantasy was Robert. Her schoolwork began to slide drastically, her depression grew much more severe, and she began to seem very different to her parents than before the incident.

Her mother and father became alarmed. They were aware of the name their daughter was acquiring in the community. They were also worried about Anna's infatuation with Robert because they were aware that the young man had acquired quite a reputation as a "lady-killer." From their point of view, he was from the worst part of town, the child of a totally unsuitable family, and not at all the one for their daughter. They worried that

Anna's blossoming figure, her spoiled reputation, and her own infatuation could lead to only one thing when Robert finally noticed her. Seeing no other option, they sent her away to school for a year—to Kentucky with her eldest brother, Mitchell, who had gotten a job as a teacher.

Depressed to the depths of her soul, Anna dutifully followed her parents' wishes. But as time passed she realized that she was no better off in Kentucky. Before too long she found herself just as hated by the girls and not trusted to be around the boys. To make matters worse, one of Anna's teachers made it her personal responsibility to discipline this wayward child, causing the girl great misery. Before too long, Anna was experiencing all of the horrors she had back home, but she was even worse off because Robert had remained behind. As her state of mind deteriorated, her teacher saw it as a rebellious spirit and rode Anna mercilessly. The discipline seemed to have no effect on the girl, so by midwinter the teacher managed to have Anna expelled.

It would have been disastrous to return home expelled because it would only confirm her reputation of corruptness in the community. Her parents were heartbroken and couldn't understand how they had managed to raise such a child. Seeing no other choice, they advised her to remain in Kentucky—being passed among relatives until the school term had ended. No one would ever have to know of her shame at school. It would be safe to come home when the school term was finally over.

The rest of the year went slowly, but eventually she found herself back at her parents'. Even after returning home, however, life never returned to normal. She just had to get away. Without her parents' knowledge, at the age of seventeen she eloped with Robert. It would become just one more heartbreak in their experience.

From the very start, Anna felt out of place with Robert's family. Her parents had been right; the families really were from two different worlds. Her only solution was to try to make the best of a difficult situation. More than anything else she wanted children, and she was bound and determined to make the marriage work.

Robert, however, seemed different after they married. He saw himself very much as the center of the universe. To make matters worse, many of Robert's friends seemed to think as highly of him as he did. It was as if he had an entourage of supporters who fell in line to wait on his every command. He appeared to get much for little, behaving as though the world owed him a living and all he had to do was wait for it. Much of the time Anna felt like an outsider in this widening circle of her husband's friends. However, each time she reached the depths of her depression, he threw just enough attention her way to keep her secure.

As time went on, her unhappiness about Robert and his family worsened. She experienced much sorrow and ill-health over a tubal pregnancy. Then the bottom fell out of her world when she realized Robert was seeing other women! It wasn't long before he didn't even try to keep it a secret. She was shamed.

Anna was totally and undeniably lost. More than anything she felt completely connected to Robert, and yet he could not or would not change. All her life she had only wanted to be a wife and a mother. When her marriage collapsed in divorce, she collapsed as well.

After a brief stay at her parents', she knew she had to leave the area. The pull Robert had on her was unbelievable. Regardless of what he had done, she couldn't get him out of her mind. Her mental health sank so low that she moved to New York to live with Vera! They worked out a deal: Anna would pay all the bills and the rent, and

Vera would finish school. In return, Anna would have a place to stay and Vera would repay half of the money to Anna as soon as it was feasible. To lessen their expenses, the two sisters took a third girl as a roommate.

Although Anna tried briefly to get a job as a singer—she had a beautiful voice—she ended up as a waitress. Nightly she would bring home her tips and keep them in a box. After a while, however, she noticed that the money seemed to be disappearing with regularity. To convince herself about what was happening, she began keeping careful track. Before too long she discovered that she was right and even caught the thief in the act. It should have come as quite a surprise to Anna to find that it wasn't the third roommate taking her money, but her own sister!

The incident was brushed aside. Later, when the two of them were rooming alone and Vera had gotten a job in a different restaurant, they agreed to split all of their earnings fifty-fifty. For a long while, Vera brought home no more than $5.00 per day. The elder girl claimed that $5.00 was the best she could do even on "a good day." However, eventually Anna had to substitute for a period of time because Vera became ill. The younger woman was shocked to find that even on some of the slowest days she averaged $18.00. It turned out that the elder sister had been pocketing the extra money all along. Vera felt that anything she could take from Anna was her due; it never seemed to bother her conscience.

Finally, Anna met a man she decided to marry. She wasn't infatuated with him and she didn't love him—that place still belonged to Robert. However, she wanted a family and felt that she was running out of time; besides, he really seemed to want her.

Vera couldn't stand to be in the same room with Anna and her fiancé, Alan. Though Vera seemed to like Alan, and she and Anna were getting along as well as could be expected, she refused to be part of a threesome. The situation didn't improve much after Alan and Anna were married; all that changed was that Vera supported Alan in everything he did and continued to find fault with everything about Anna.

Alan couldn't find work in New York, so Anna returned home with him, where her father tried to set Alan up with a job. Anna's desire to be with Robert had not subsided, so she was thankful that his life had taken him in a direction where their paths did not cross. For a time Anna thought everything would turn out for the best, but it soon appeared that she was wrong.

Her marriage became unbearable. She didn't love her husband and at times resented the fact that they were together. When she was unhappiest, she fantasized that Robert would return and take her away. As miserable as she had been with Robert, she couldn't get him out of her mind. She only stayed with Alan for the sake of having children; she was nearly thirty years old and running out of time.

One of her darkest moments came when her physical condition indicated another tubal pregnancy. She felt defeated and lost. She was unhappy with Alan and hopelessly connected to Robert. She had been referred to Edgar Cayce by several friends. Prior to visiting Mr. Cayce she had thrown herself to the floor sobbing, wishing to die. It was nearly the end of January 1938, and though she thought her life over, it was about to change dramatically.

In order to verify for herself the authenticity of Mr. Cayce's clairvoyance, she did not tell him of her problem nor did she mention her previous operation. She merely stated that she needed a physical reading. Although desperate for help, she was quite suspect of this psychic business and had pursued the possibility only at the insistence of one of her friends.

Her doubts were laid to rest, however, when Mr. Cayce, in the midst of the reading while "asleep" on the couch, uttered one sentence: " . . . disturbances with the activities of the pelvic organs, and as in the present there is the false conception that has produced in the tube that is left—there's one . . . " Because of the tone of the overall reading and its undeniable accuracy, she followed Cayce's suggestions to the letter, which included a change of diet, internal medications, and massage; within two weeks there was vast improvement and within two months she felt physically normal. No operation was necessary.

In April of that year she had her first life reading, and its information transformed the way she thought about herself, her hardships, and her family. Cayce began the reading by stating, "Yes, we have the records here of that entity now known as or called [Anna Campbell]." (1523-4) Although Anna had never even considered something as foreign to her as reincarnation, the insights she gained from the reading changed her life forever and became as real to her as the present. Anna would later tell Mr. Cayce that having come in contact with him and his family meant "more to me than anything that has ever come into my existence . . . " for the past seemed connected to the present in the most remarkable way. The story which emerged from the Akashic Records contained striking connections to her present-day problems.

A hundred years previously, she had been born as a daughter into the household of a frontier family. Her parents were settlers who tried hard to eke a living from the land. Apparently, at the time, Anna was interested most in herself, not caring for the lifestyle advocated by her nineteenth-century parents. Her reading summed up Anna's motivation during that period as "What she desired she took; what she wanted she got!"

In an interesting preview of her present, when she was seventeen, an unsuitable drifter convinced her to run away from home as his "companion." She agreed without hesitation, and the two journeyed westward to an area then known as Fort Dearborn, near present-day Chicago.

Before long, she was befriended by a saloon madam who owned one of the taverns. The woman was a great source of help and inspiration to many of the girls who worked for her. In fact, the elder woman helped many of them get back on the right track when their life seemed darkest. The madam saw their work as a way of giving companionship to lonely men and a means of giving women time to reconsider their lives. On the other hand, Anna saw it as a way of obtaining whatever she wanted. In spite of their different approaches, the madam would become her dearest friend and closest advisor—and her own mother one hundred years in the future. By choice, Anna became an entertainer in the tavern and didn't hesitate to provide private amusement to the saloon's clients. In time, she had a child fathered by her drifter-companion, though she insisted on retaining her position as entertainer, waitress, and bar moll.

Except for one of the fort's guides, few problems seemed to impinge upon her life. The guide, a self-styled minister, was abhorred by the "abominations" that occurred within the tavern. In contrast, he found his life to be rather exemplary. Because of his judgments about the inappropriateness of what was occurring, he found frequent occasion to condemn the tavern's activities, its entertainers, and even its patrons. This led to frequent confrontations (and fistfights!) between Anna's drifter-companion and the guide. A number of times the guide had the tar whipped out of him, and the conflict between the two was never really settled: it was no surprise to Anna to find that her drifter-companion would return as her brother, Warren, and the fort's guide was none other than her pa.

Eventually, Anna's nineteenth-century counterpart grew tired of her relationship with the drifter and took up with a frontiersman named John Bainbridge. Life remained pretty much the same until Indian attacks on the fort caused Bainbridge and Anna and a group of others to escape. During one attack and the ensuing escape, Anna was forced to abandon her child. Although having no choice in the matter, Anna apparently never gave the child a second thought—it would provide for an interesting turnabout in the next century when all she could think about was children and wonder why she was barren.

Indians pursued the group, at one point surrounding them as they drifted through the slow-moving waters of a river. Becoming very afraid, Anna had a reoccurring thought throughout the episode: "I've got to get out of this place. I've got to get out of this place!" That same thought would be repeated in her aunt's house when a scene would call the memory to mind after the fort, the Indians, and the danger had long ceased to exist.

Finally, Anna managed to escape from the Indians; Bainbridge would lose his life saving hers. Eventually, she would end up in Virginia, the place of her "current nativity." With her arrival in Virginia, she became a new person. Perhaps it was the events of her early life or perhaps it was her desire to start over, but whatever the cause, Anna became known as an "angel" to those in need. She comforted the sick, counseled the wayward, and assisted the poor. Her life touched many and she was held in great esteem for her kindness—no one would know of her bar-moll adventures.

At one point, she nursed back to health a settler who

seemed emotionally neglected by his wife. The end result was that he fell in love with her and abandoned his own wife. Anna took to him not so much because she loved him, but because he loved her and no longer would she look out only for herself. Interestingly, though the man's wife wasn't interested in him, she didn't want anyone else to be interested either. She became extremely bitter, mostly toward Anna for stealing something that was "hers." One hundred years later the bitter wife would become Anna's sister, Vera, and the man she didn't really love would return as her second husband, Alan.

Though her nineteenth-century life was not long in duration—she died at forty-eight—it entailed a great many adventures, experiences, and lessons, all of which would have a direct bearing on her next life when she would be born into a frontier family in a very small town in the twentieth century.

The Dearborn experience was not the only lifetime given to Anna by Cayce; however, it was reported as the greatest influence on her current sojourn. She was told of two additional lifetimes recorded upon the records that were having a tremendous influence on her present: one in France and one in Laodicea (part of the Roman Empire). All told, Anna was given six lifetimes that were greatly affecting her present experience: Fort Dearborn, France, Laodicea, Israel, Egypt, and Atlantis. It was France that had set up the situation with her first husband, Robert.

In France they had been lovers, where it was a well-kept secret. Robert had been one of the nobility and Catholic and unable to obtain a divorce. Out of necessity and on infrequent occasions, she had become his mistress. She would spend a lifetime desiring to be with him.

Unfortunately, although being with him was her sole desire, it was not his. Being of the nobility, he had grown to love the pomp and the elegance and the respect that his position provided. He loved walking into a room and watching heads turn to meet his gaze; he loved having an entourage follow after him, waiting on his every word; he loved possessing women who would throw themselves at him, wishing to be a part of his world. All these things would follow him for two hundred years—affording him situations that would seem rather unusual when measured against his twentieth-century status and lack of education.

The reading made it clear that much of Anna's infatuation with Robert was because she had desired and continued to desire a perfect relationship with him. It also hinted at the fact that this was only a desire and not a real likelihood; yet it was a desire not to be easily overcome.

Her reading stated that she would experience "greater harmony" in her life lasting "until '40 and '41, when AGAIN there will be a period of disturbance." The reading urged her to continue working on her relationship with her current husband, Alan, even stating that it would be possible to conceive a child if they could only work things out. Regardless of the possibility of children, however, there were definite reasons the two of them were together. The reading provided Anna with insights she could work with, though she rarely discussed any of the information with anyone, including members of her own family.

During the 1930s and 1940s, the topic of past lives and reincarnation was not one which often occurred across the breakfast table. On a number of occasions, her family members would go to Mr. Cayce for a physical reading, and they got help. In fact, Vera would eventually be cured of tuberculosis (but she refused to get a life reading), and Mitchell's firstborn would be saved from a life-threatening illness. Even then only a few seemed open to the specifics of reincarnation, and some weren't interested at all in hearing about what went on at Mr. Cayce's home. For Anna, the information was all factual and enabled her to piece together the lives of those closest to her. As brief examples, she learned the following about her parents:

In addition to being the fort's guide in Dearborn, her father had been a tax collector in Rome and an inspector of military garrisons. This existence had caused him to become rather severe in his dealings with others, and the severity would remain with him nearly 1,900 years later as the father of six children. An interesting out-of-character quality that Anna had always noticed in her father was his ability to pick out clothing and fine cloth; it amazed her that he could buy a dress or a coat for her, or her sister, or her mother that was perfect. According to the Akashic Records, he had been a merchant of fine material in Persia. In Egypt, he was known for his fine workmanship in the construction of homes—as he would be centuries later in Virginia. Connected with members of his family throughout time, he had known his wife in Dearborn, Palestine, and Egypt, and Anna in Dearborn, Egypt, and Persia. Recognizing that he was often judgmental and severe, the records also stated that he was a great leader and motivator of people, as well as talented in workmanship. The advice given him by the reading was that he should begin practicing the devout and spiritual life he had so frequently preached.

As the kindly madam in the Dearborn experience, Anna's mother had been associated, one way or another, with all of her children. Her ability to always know what to say or to prepare individuals for a new life—an ability that had been most evidenced in Dearborn—had been cultivated in ancient Egypt. Apparently it had been her duty as a teacher to help prepare emissaries and teachers to other lands. Interestingly enough, she had been a teacher before her marriage to Anna's father this time around. Her most influential life had been one in Palestine—several of her current children had also been her children then. In that life she had also experienced a healing from Jesus Himself! From that same time period she had developed her hatred of Catholics: she had been a member of the apostle Peter's household and had known the apostle Paul. Firsthand, she had witnessed how the message of this Man, Jesus, had been nearly lost by the Church's early contention between these two—the 2,000-year-old frustration was still carried within her heart. The reading stated that in addition to her other talents, she was adept at healing and at growing plants—a flower business would appear in 1941, after her children had been raised.

It's worth noting the different karmic effect that the bar-moll occupation had on both Anna and her mother, because it's apparently not the deed of prostitution that created karma for Anna but the reasons behind it. As a dance-hall girl, Anna felt she could get anything she wanted personally; on the other hand, Anna's mother saw her occupation as a means of helping others. A hundred years later the effect was that Anna's mother retained her ability to help others, whereas Anna was still labeled a loose woman. From Cayce's perspective, it wasn't **the deed** with which the Akashic Records were most concerned; rather, it was **the intent** (the real purpose) behind that deed.

Anna worked diligently on her relationship with Alan, all the while remembering the ominous prediction about " '40 and '41" contained in her reading. In an effort to prepare herself for the inevitable, she procured another reading and asked, " . . . please explain just what this refers to, and . . . how may I best prepare myself for it and meet it correctly?" The answer was, "To give as to what such would be, would not be in keeping with the entity using self's OWN will, self's own choice or judgment." (1523-11) The reading went on to say that there remained much she needed to work on with Alan, hinting that if it wasn't taken care of in this life, she would have to fulfill it in another.

One year later the prediction came true. Without warning, despite the intervening years and seemingly out of the blue, Robert would return to her and want the two of them to get back together. The desire she felt for him was almost overpowering, though logic and common sense agreed that it would never work. He said he had changed; she knew he could not. And yet she was not happy with Alan, and her unhappiness made her want Robert all the more. In desperation she asked in a reading if this was the event that had been predicted. The response was affirmative, stating that the situation was to become even more tempting. It did. Apparently the cycle of her French incarnation had rolled around once more.

Although it was one of the hardest things she would ever do, she ignored Robert's advances and pushed aside the urge to become his mistress. They had many opportunities to be together, but while together they simply talked. She was torn between her desire to be with him and her attempts to work things out with Alan. Time passed, and she continued to do what her head said was right, even though it caused her heart great difficulty. Eventually, Robert entered the service and was again out of the picture, though the two would be in frequent correspondence throughout World War II. Ultimately, she overcame her desire to be with him, though Anna would feel love toward Robert for the rest of her life.

The years slipped by, and Anna never had the children she wanted. She tried to save her marriage with Alan, but her effort didn't work—though in the end she was thankful they had managed to stay together for as long as they had; in the process each of them had learned a great deal. She would marry again, but never have any children. It probably came as just one more heartbreak to find that both Robert and Alan would eventually father children with their next wives.

Happily, a child did enter Anna's family, becoming an integral part of her life. He was Billy, her brother Carl's son. She spent much time with him, playing and going to the beach. She had several "happenings" with the child that convinced her they had known one another before. Oftentimes, she pretended he was "her son," even allowing strangers they encountered to assume likewise. The closeness she felt toward him was experienced in return by the child. Oftentimes Billy threatened his parents by saying he was going to live with Anna, for he loved her "the very best." Later, a reading confirmed that Billy had been her son in Laodicea and his father at the time was the same man who would become John Bainbridge, Anna's second companion in Dearborn 1,900 years later.

Her relationship with Billy would always be close. Just as his own mother was Catholic, Billy would become Catholic and go to parochial school and somehow Anna's own mother would survive it all. Unfortunately, however, Billy and his father had a very difficult time getting along. Apparently his father and mother had also been married in Dearborn, and Billy had been present as well. Most of Anna's family, it seemed, were playing out their Dearborn cycle.

In Dearborn as a priest, Billy had been horrified to see his sister (his present mother) married and taken away by a man he found unworthy and inappropriate (his present father). It was jealousy, to be sure. However, the priest's affections for his sister were genuinely deep because the two had been companions in France as well as mother and son in Egypt. This jealousy was very difficult for both father and son to work out. Billy's father claimed that his marriage had been happy and ideal until the birth of his son. Billy's father, Carl, was eventually transferred to Chicago! Perhaps it was best that the problems be dealt with and solved in the very place they had arisen.

Years later, Billy would confirm one of the past-life scenarios Edgar Cayce had taken from the Akashic Records. While he was a priest in the Dearborn experience, Billy's reading stated he had ministered to the needs of the frontier's people. In Chicago, while his seventh-grade class studied the frontier and the white man's westward migration, Billy provided information that surprised his teacher, a nun. The lesson centered around a priest who had been helpful to an Indian chief in preventing a massacre. Billy suddenly called out the name of the Indian. His response startled the nun because the name of the chief, although known to her, was not contained in the textbook. She inquired as to how he knew, and his response was that he had been a priest and had lived in that part of the country and knew of the Indian. Though his answer had been correct, she didn't have the slightest idea what he was talking about.

For the rest of her life, Anna would attempt to share with others much of what she had found in the Cayce readings. Perhaps because she had firsthand experience, she became an avid proponent of the health readings. She would have more than her share of opportunities to care for the declining health of members of her own family. Possibly because her Dearborn cycle of "comforting the sick" had rolled around once more, or because, in meeting self, she was overcoming the Dearborn tendency to care of only her own needs, or both, she spent years nursing both parents through their old age and was with each one when they died. In time, she would have to care for a third husband and eventually her sister Vera as each passed through old age, sickness, and death. In fact, she would spend nearly twenty years of her life taking care of at least one person or another totally dependent upon her!

She never had any doubt about the validity of the material in the readings. Throughout her life she had found more than just physical help from the information, for one by one her trying relationships had improved: her relationship with herself, with Robert, and even with Alan took on a whole new meaning because of the information Cayce pulled from records. Perhaps the most difficult relationship, however, was Anna's relationship with Vera. Just as it would be the first one to cause Anna the most difficulty, it would be the last one to be resolved—a process taking more than seventy years.

In 1946, a psychologist named Gina Cerminara was piecing together information on reincarnation from the Cayce files. Her work would eventually evolve into the bestselling book, *Many Mansions*. While researching the information, Dr. Cerminara inquired about the relationship between Anna and her sister, Vera. A portion of Anna's response from August 7, 1946, is as follows:

> Dear Gina:
>   Probably the best way to write up the report you requested is to picture myself talking to you. My spelling is lousy and I'm pretty much out of practice writing—but here goes!
>   The disharmony between [Vera] and me started at a very early age. The first incident I remember took place when I was about eight and [Vera] fourteen. Two cousins (girls about the same ages as

ours) visited us for a few days. I suppose it isn't at all uncommon for kids to clash but somehow this seemed to stand out in my mind. Any attention I would get annoyed [Vera] to the point that she would whip up all kinds of imaginary things, such as pretending that she was going somewhere or that she had toys to play with, and if they wanted to share these things with her—they would have to leave me out of it. I was no match for her then and she usually won her point. I wasn't conscious of having any feeling of antagonism at that age, but I would feel hurt and defeated and most often would end up playing by myself and of course feeling very sorry for myself. Envy seemed to be the outstanding feeling at that time . . . Mama got so she didn't pay any attention to us but just let us fight it out.

After I was separated from [Robert] and before I married [Alan] we spent three winters together. Beginning then, another outstanding characteristic presented itself and has stayed with us right along. She always felt quite free to take anything that was mine—first without my knowing it and eventually it didn't matter whether I knew it or not . . . Since she felt that I had taken [Alan] away from her—even though the readings indicated that was not the case—she undoubtedly came back this time with the feeling that anything she could take from me was her due—for it certainly never seemed to bother her conscience . . .

I firmly believe I fulfilled my obligations with [Alan] for this incarnation. Not so with [Vera]— there will be more to come—and so this report is only complete to date, perhaps not complete but sufficient, I hope . . .

Case 1523-11 Report File

After their roommate days, Vera did marry, although it would be disastrous for her. Eventually she would divorce and return to her parents' home. In spite of Vera's presence, however, when her parents' health began to decline, it was Anna who shouldered the greatest responsibility for their care. Although this fact caused Anna some frustration, it also provided for a decade of opportunities to begin working with Vera and their own mixed feelings on a regular basis. With a great deal of effort on both parts the relationship between the two sisters became "tolerable." It was this feeling that eventually replaced the feelings of distrust and animosity. However, just being "tolerable" would not finish their work together.

Through a chain of life events and family moves and deaths, late in life Anna and Vera found themselves thrown together as each other's closest relative. When nearly an octogenarian, Vera became bedridden with no one to care for her except Anna who was in her seventies. The situation lasted for two years, and although Anna had nursing assistance in caring for her sister, in a very real sense they had many opportunities to be alone together and talk and reminisce and think of days gone by. Toward the end of Vera's life it seemed as though all animosity that had existed between them was finally gone. In fact, two days before she died, with words carrying great emotion and sincerity Vera whispered to Anna, "I hope we can be sisters again." Finally, there had been a reconciliation.

Years after Mr. Cayce's death, Anna provided yet another reincarnation confirmation regarding an episode that had occurred with her brother, Warren. He was the brother who had been her drifter-companion in the dance hall days of Dearborn, he was the one family member least interested in the Cayce phenomena, and the one who knew absolutely nothing about reincarnation. Her report says it all:

> I went dancing for a couple of hours at the American Legion, in a party with [Warren] and his wife and friends. [Warren] was so obviously in his Dearborn background, going from table to table, patting different ones on the back, drinking, etc. He came back to the table and started in asking me to sing his favorite number . . . wanting me to sing with the band, insisting that he would stand right there by me and hold my hand. Said he loved me better than anyone else in the world—and had been trying to figure out why he hadn't married me (this in a laughing vein, of course). Said he would rather dance with me than anyone else he'd ever danced with. That is of particular interest in view of the fact that he knows nothing of his connection with me in Dearborn—in fact rejects anything that deals with the thought of reincarnation . . .
>
> Case 1523-11 Report File

In a very real sense, Anna's present came into marvelous perspective when viewed from the past. By her own account, she was able to come to a clearer understanding of herself and every member of her family simply because of the reincarnation information contained within the Akashic Records. From a philosophical perspective it was life-changing, but in a very real sense the information gave her practical insights into herself and others—insights that enabled Anna to deal with necessary situations in this process of "meeting" herself.

In spite of a lifetime of many hardships, Anna would spend her remaining years in excellent health, financial security, and great optimism. Nearly identical to her

Dearborn days, she would become a "counselor." Because of her knowledge of the Cayce readings, hundreds would seek her out for help, advice, or simply someone with whom they could talk. Individuals from all walks of life found her insights extremely helpful, never really knowing the extent in which Anna's own background and trials had molded her. People often found her a source of inspiration, compassion, and understanding. Once again, the cycle would roll around and she would be seen as "an angel," possessing the innate ability to be of great help and assistance to others.

3

Recognizing Insights
from Your Own Past

———•———

$\mathcal{F}$rom Edgar Cayce's perspective, the Akashic Records maintain an infinite variety of data from the past. Whether it's the previous lives of a specific individual or the unrecorded history of an ancient civilization, all manner of information is stored and available to anyone who can access the database. Cayce's own access to the material seemed limitless, detailing everything from an individual soul's sojourn through space and time to long narratives regarding ancient history and long-forgotten civilizations. Regardless of the query, Edgar Cayce seemed adept at obtaining the records.

At the beginning of readings about the past, Cayce would often focus on specific incidents that occurred during the individual's present lifetime. Sometimes this

focus detailed long-forgotten accidents or childhood
traumas. On other occasions, he might discuss early
present-day experiences that seemed relevant in an
individual's life at the moment. In the life readings—
those readings dealing with the subject of past lives—
Edgar Cayce would go back over the years from the present,
briefly mentioning the years back to the individual's
birth. For example, in a 1937 life reading, given to a
woman who had been born in 1883, the reading stated:

> Edgar Cayce: [In going back over the years from the
> time the reading was given] 1931—such a diffusion
> of interests!—'30, '29—'18—such anxieties!—'17—
> '98—yes, a change again in surroundings—'88—
> '83—How happy they [parents] were to have the
> entity!
> We have the record here of that entity now known
> as or called [1479].
>
> 1479-1

Invariably, after acquiring the records for the individual in question, Cayce would discuss "astrological influences" that seemed relevant in the individual's life.
Unique in its approach, the reading by Cayce offered an
interesting look at how astrology and the soul were
somehow connected.

The Cayce material suggests that our lives are not governed by the planets because we were born at such a
time in a certain place, but rather we are born into the
earth—surrounded by the planets—at a time and place
which materially represents who we are at a soul level.
In other words, Cayce states that "the universe stood
still" (3003-1) at the exact moment of a child's birth. At
that particular moment in time, the planets create a
unique, physical astrological representation of whom

this soul is innately and spiritually. For this reason, Cayce believed that a study of astrology could give an individual a fairly accurate indication of the qualities, traits, opportunities, and challenges that *he or she came in with*—some of the same information that is available from the records themselves. However, because free will is the single strongest influence in an individual's life, it would not be as straightforward to use astrology to equate *where the individual was going*. In the language of the readings:

> . . . no action of any planet or any of the phases of the Sun, Moon, or any of the heavenly bodies surpass the rule of Man's individual will power—the power given by the Creator of man in the beginning, when he became a living soul, with the power of choosing for himself.
>
> 254-2

Another interesting concept that Cayce acquired from the Akashic Records was that in between an individual's earthly physical lives, a soul experiences "planetary sojourns in consciousness." These sojourns enable a soul to learn focused lessons (such as unconditional love) before returning to the earth with a hopefully expanded awareness. This does not suggest that individuals go to other planets in the solar system; instead, the readings indicate that each of the planets is simply a physical representation of a corresponding state of consciousness.

Individuals who received life readings from Edgar Cayce were told what planetary influences had affected them prior to their present earthly incarnation and how these states of consciousness had impacted their inner characteristics. According to the readings, these sojourns in consciousness manifest as strong, unconscious influences on an individual's personality, character, urges, desires, habits, and even preferences.

For example, in the case of a forty-six-year-old male who wanted a life reading, Cayce gained access to the Akashic Records and then discussed the "latent and manifested" urges that were present because of planetary sojourns and astrological influences. Cayce was told that the individual had been born on June 29, 1893—erroneous information which would quickly be corrected. The reading said, in part:

> Edgar Cayce: [In going back over years from the present—"—'37—periods of activity that are not so good—'31—disturbing forces, and yet good determinations that fell down—'21—expectancies—" etc., on back to birth date. Then: "28th rather than the 29th, as we find; though it was late in the day, the time being close to the change, yet 28th."]
>
> We have the records here of that entity now known as or called [2172].
>
> In giving the interpretations of the records as we find them, these are chosen with the desire and purpose that this be a helpful experience for the entity.
>
> While there may be interpretations of virtues and faults, these are pointed out that there may be the greater realization to the entity that the entrance into this experience in the earth is purposeful; that it is not by chance but rather that the infinite mercy of the Creative Forces, God, may be so manifested that the entity may take hope—not lose hope, as it has; or attempt to run away from self, in attempting to smother or cover up that consciousness or the fear which finds expression at times in the experiences.
>
> For, self-indulgence—or the running away from

self—gains nothing; only creating, bringing about in the experience that which is at times hard to meet; and one becomes discouraged at its own efforts, and oft begins to condemn someone else for those disturbances which may have arisen.

Know that there is a purpose; a way, a manner in which self may come to the greater realization of what the Creative Force, or God, has for thee to do in this experience . . .

In giving the interpretations of the records that are written upon the skein of time and space, by the activities of the entity upon or in conscious influence or action . . .

We find that the sojourns upon the planets during the interims between the material or earthly manifestations have a part in the urges latent and manifested in the experience of this entity, as in every entity.

It is true that from the astrological aspects the entity has diverted and is diverting some of the manifested urges. Yet, know that no urge, no sign, no emotion—whether of a latent mental nature or of a material or emotional nature finding expression in the body—surpasses that birthright, WILL—the factor which makes the human soul, the human individual, DIFFERENT from all other creatures in the earth, from all manifestations of God's activity!

For he, man, has been made just a little lower than the angels; with all the abilities to become ONE WITH HIM! not the whole, nor yet lost in the individuality of the whole, but becoming more and more personal in ALL of its consciousnesses of the application of the individuality of Creative Forces, thus more and more at-onement with Him—yet conscious of being himself.

From the astrological sojourns we find these as rather the influences in the experience:

Jupiter—the benevolent influence, indicating the activities of the entity as being mostly among its fellow men, APPLIED in INDIVIDUAL ways, yet affecting in its relationships rather the masses or groups in their activities.

Hence the individual activity of the entity should be in any expression in the material plane dealing with individuals' emotions and individuals' activities, rather than with things; though it is possible that THROUGH things used by individuals there would be the greater expression—whether in the demonstrating, or in the activity as a salesman OF such . . .

Mercury—these influences are indicated in a manner, or character, or way of thinking. Yet the entity has allowed itself to drift somewhat away from this ability to make decisions . . .

Arouse self, then, to that ability to "think straight" on subjects, on conditions, on activities; not so much in a speculative way or manner—for, while there have been periods when apparently things went well, even in this sojourn, know that ye are but meeting thyself—and things appear not so well . . .

Neptune—from this sojourn we find influences pertaining to things of the mystical nature. Hence the inclination for the entity to be speculative, or to speculate in ways that may not always be wise.

But IF the activities are in relationships with peoples, having to do with things that come over, or pass through, or grow in water, then much more easily will there be found harmony in the activities—if the speculative influences will be resisted oft in the experience.

From the astrological sojourns, then, we find

both good and bad influences, TO BE SURE; but the outcome of such is dependent upon what is the ideal in relationships to things, to individuals, to purposes, to spiritual imports.

2172-1

Once the Akashic Records had been accessed, and once Cayce had explored the planetary influences affecting the individual, the past lives most impacting the present would be explored.

Frequently, when individuals begin discussing the possibilities of their own past lives, they may theorize a connection between themselves and some famous historical personage. Sometimes they may even believe they were that person. Critics of reincarnation often joke that everyone was a Cleopatra, or a Caesar, or an apostle, a Founding Father, or some king or queen from history. Whatever happened to all the peasants and serfs and everyday ordinary people?

The reincarnation files of the Edgar Cayce readings are literally filled with more than ten thousand names of individuals from the past. Of that number, less than two hundred have been identified as being "famous." Although such names as Aaron Burr and Anne Boleyn are contained within the files, "famous characters" also include such personages as "Socrates' daughter" and "a relative of Sam Houston." To be sure, most individuals who had reincarnation readings from Edgar Cayce were ordinary people in the past.

One commonly overlooked aspect of the "famous-person syndrome" is that individuals may be responding to patterns of human experience and behavior rather than literal past-life identities. Very often, an individual in the present resonates to someone famous in history, not because he or she was that person but because the notable figure represents or corresponds to something in the individual's present lifetime. Another possibility is that a person's present-day connection with a past-life identity is not because the person was that individual, but rather because the present-day person was once familiar with that famous individual. One example from the readings is the case of a forty-seven-year-old man (1151-4) who was convinced he was the reincarnation of President James A. Garfield. This connection had even been confirmed by another psychic. However, Cayce stated that the individual had simply been a very close associate of Garfield's, and not the president himself.

A thirty-two-year-old woman asked Edgar Cayce about whether or not a person she knew had ever been famous in a past life. The response she received provides additional verification regarding the significance of each soul's identity rather than the human personality which may be presently manifesting:

> Q. Was he any famous or well-known entity in a past incarnation?
> A. What entity is NOT famous! What entity is NOT well known in the end! As to being worldly famous—no more than in the present; as a teacher, a helper to those along life's seeking way.
>
> 2072-10

From Cayce's perspective, every individual was very much an integral portion of the whole. Ultimately, the purpose of each lifetime was to undergo experiences which would enable the soul to become more in tune with its divine origins. Whether or not that ideal was actually achieved became a matter of free will, but regardless of the specific lifetime, the opportunity for soul growth was ever present.

Whenever Edgar Cayce read the Akashic Records for an individual, much of it dealt with the individual's past in this present life. For example, a middle-aged man who had immigrated from Russia asked for a life reading in 1935 (619-5). He was unsure of his exact age (listing it as "about 48") or date of birth. Cayce tuned in to the records and, once again, began a reading by providing the man with his correct birth information: *March 19, 1885*, making the individual two years older than he had previously thought. In another instance, which would become one of the most celebrated cases of Cayce's early career, the Akashic Records correctly pinpointed the mental dysfunction and physical convulsions of a six-year-old girl (2473-1) to a fall and an illness she had experienced at the age of two.

During the forty-three years he gave readings, it became repeatedly clear to Edgar Cayce that the Akashic Records contained a limitless array of information. Access to that information, however, frequently seemed bounded by specific guidelines and parameters. In addition to the fact that an individual's interpretation of the Akashic Records could be shaded by his or her intent, purposes, and belief systems, Cayce also suggested that an intuitive would have an easier time accessing information about a soul's historical past if that intuitive had also been incarnate in the earth during that same time period. A 1934 reading explained this principle as follows:

Then, this body through whom the information comes being in accord or attune, by the subjugation of consciousness into materiality, becomes the channel through which such records may be read.

The interpretation of the records, then, depends upon how good a reader the body is, or how well in accord with the varied experiences through which the entity seeking has passed—or the records that have been made by that soul. **Hence, there may be much more of a detailed record read of an experience through which both souls passed, than of environs that were not a portion of that soul so interpreting the activities.**

But each soul as this, [416], has made a definite record just as clear as that which may be written with ink and pen or with any other type, style or form of transmitting or recording that activity of an individual soul. [Author's emphasis] 416-2

Compounding the uncertainty of obtaining accurate information from the Akashic Records is the fact that Cayce stated it was sometimes very difficult to tell the difference between a thought and a deed (1562-1). A corollary of this idea is contained in Scripture when Jesus announces that to lust after an individual is the same as committing the act (Matthew 5:28). Since the availability of information from the Akashic Records was not always straightforward, did the Cayce readings suggest methods of obtaining insights from one's past that could be relied upon? The answer is yes.

In 1932, while giving past-life reading 2741-1, the unconscious Cayce had a dream in which he saw a great number of people going to dedicate a pyramid. Apparently, there was a magnificent ceremony that included seven days of entertainment, dancing, song, and celebration. Cayce recalled having seen camels, and people attired in the costume of ancient Egypt. When he awoke from the reading, he related the dream to those around him. A subsequent reading (294-131) stated that Cayce's dream had been an actual happening from the past—a happening which Cayce himself had witnessed. In other words, in the dream state, an individual's subconscious mind gains access to everything from that person's past. Confirming the availability of past-life insights in this manner, a thirty-two-year-old woman was told that whenever a dream of some past time frame repeated itself she could consider it a literal "experience in turning back in time and space" (2072-12). Therefore, if individuals find a number of their dreams occurring in Colonial America, for example, they could be fairly certain there was a life experience at that time in history.

A contemporary case of past-life recall in the dream state includes the story of a man and a woman, Michael and Susan, who seemed to simultaneously remember a past-life experience when they had been together as husband and wife. At the time, Michael and Susan shared an office together as "friendly co-workers."

Michael was very much concerned about Pam, a female friend of his who was contemplating asking her husband for a divorce. Pam was convinced that she had found her "true soul mate" (not her husband) and wanted to get a divorce in order to be with that soul mate. While Pam was still considering what course to follow, Michael had the following dream:

> I dreamed that I was talking to Pam about her decision to divorce. In the dream, I told Pam that all of us have more than one "soul mate"—a soul with whom we have been together. I then turned and pointed to Susan, who was in the same room, and said, "You see, Pam, in my last life I was married to Susan" and yet now we are just friends. It wouldn't be right for me to run off with Susan this time around."

Michael awoke from the dream on a Saturday morning and decided to tell Susan about it when he returned to work on Monday. That same weekend, Susan was going for a drive in the mountains with her husband. She related her experience as follows:

> My husband, Tim, was driving and I was enjoying the beautiful scenery. All at once, I saw the most gorgeous sunset. I looked at it and seemed to be transported to another space and time. For some reason, it felt as if I were seeing Austria (even though we were driving in the mountains of Virginia). Suddenly, the thought came to me to remember what I was seeing so that I could relate the experience back to my husband (who was Michael in my mind!) when I returned home.

On Monday morning, at work, Michael and Susan shared their past-life experiences with each other.

In addition to dreams, according to Edgar Cayce, there is a very strong correlation between the imagination and one's intuition. In fact, he stated that anyone who is imaginative is intuitive. Sometimes an individual may have an unusual idea or a thought that comes from out of the blue and perhaps that individual may even say, "That's only my imagination," when, in fact, the information may be an accurate psychic impression from the Akashic Records. For example, in 1944, Cayce gave a past-life reading to a fifty-year-old woman and mentioned a life she had lived just previously in the state of Ohio—the same state as her current nativity. Later, the woman wrote and described an experience she had once had as a child:

> . . . I feel I must tell you of an incident that occurred when I was somewhere around twelve to

fourteen. We lived on a garden farm that had come to my father as the eldest son, entailed property that had passed from father to son unbroken for at least four generations, upon which was the brick house I mentioned before. I loved to accompany my father on his jaunts about the countryside and on this occasion he was driving the farm wagon several miles for some special seed wheat he had heard greatly praised.

It was a beautiful fall day and for several miles the road followed the lovely Muskingum and was entirely familiar to me. We then crossed the south side and followed the Stovertown-Cannelville road on over the hills winding through covered bridges and over little brooks, when suddenly my father swung the team to the left of a half-hidden little woodsy road that passed under a railroad and came suddenly out of the dimness into the sunlight on a beautiful green meadow; it spread before us, the bottomland, climbing gently up the hillside to where a white fence separated it from the lawn that surrounds an attractive white farmhouse with the wooded hill rising back of it. "Oh," I exclaimed delightedly, "Oh, Daddy, I know that house—I've been there lots of times." "No," my father said, "you have never been this way before." "Oh yes," I insisted. "Oh yes, Daddy" . . . My father was a very strict, stern Scotsman and his children knew better than to contradict him, and when he replied in his sternest manner, "That will do, we will hear no more of this nonsense; you have never driven any place except with me and I have never driven on this road before," the matter ended right there as far as he was concerned. However through all the years the picture of that place has never faded—it shines before

my eyes this minute in all its detail. I never saw it
again but I feel I have known it always, and I think if
I could have entered the door I would have been at
home. I could go to it I am sure. I believe I could
make a map that could be followed to it but to what
end I know not . . .

Case 5260-1 Report File

Since each individual is the sum total of all of his or
her previous experiences, fragments of past-life memories frequently come to the surface in everyday life. Often, however, individuals don't know how commonplace
these experiences are (such as an immediate feeling of
animosity toward a new co-worker), or they become
concerned when children, especially, discuss ideas and
experiences that are foreign to their present environment. (For further study, books such as *Twenty Cases
Suggestive of Reincarnation* by Ian Stevenson examine
examples of past-life memory experiences in children.)

Although heredity and environment might explain
our similarities with members of our family, reincarnation helps to explain the differences. We all have activities, locations, and people toward which we are drawn.
As mentioned earlier, individuals pick up relationships
exactly where they were left off the last time around. Frequently a close kinship with an individual in the present
merely reflects the ongoing relationship which has been
developed between those two people. With that in mind,
the following daydream experience might contain valid
past-life insights:

Greg and Jim were best friends who, on occasion, also
worked together in construction. The relationship between the two had been close since the day they met.
Jim had often said that "Greg is like a brother." After
working a job together, more than anything the two

looked forward to the end of the day and "sharing a six pack and just relaxing." One day while Greg was driving his truck to a job site to begin the day (and Jim was riding as passenger), Jim had an unusual experience:

I was talking to Greg, who was driving, when suddenly it was like something fell in front of my eyes, and Greg's appearance changed. Suddenly, it looked as though Greg was wearing a cowboy hat and a bola tie. He was wearing boots, as well. All at once, I *knew* Greg was my brother and I *knew* that we had gone to California for the Gold Rush. I also *knew* that we had spent most of our time going from one saloon to another, talking about getting gold but never actually finding any. I suddenly become conscious of all these images and I thought, "What the heck?!" and all at once the images were gone and I was back in the truck with Greg.

In a case from Edgar Cayce's personal life, in 1926 a child was given a reading in which it was stated that the child had once been "Thomas Cayce"—Cayce's little brother who had died when Edgar was only fifteen (318-2). Although the child was not told of the experience, he seemed to recall his connection to Mr. Cayce when the two finally met each other two years later. Cayce recalled what had happened:

He merely stood off and looked intently at me. Then, suddenly he rushed to me with his little face radiant and said, "Brother" . . . He at once began to beg me to take him home with me—that he belonged to me, that he didn't belong there. I had to leave while he was asleep . . . did not see him again until he was past ten. Then was in the home again

. . . When I went to leave, he was packed to leave
with me without saying anything. Then I tried to
talk with him, told him how necessary he was in
that home and he must finish school there. He was
resigned. Incredible story . . . but every word true,
so help me GOD! Had you had that experience,
what would you say?

Case 2722-5 Report File

In addition to watching one's dreams and spontane-
ous imaginative experiences, methods of obtaining information from the Akashic Records about one's past
may include hypnosis, getting a personal psychic reading, and personal reveries. (An example of a personal
reverie is at the end of this chapter.) Because of the many
conditions which influence an individual's access to the
Akashic Records, Cayce recommended that any information received be weighed against what an individual
already knew about himself or herself. Just because
something was "psychic" doesn't necessarily mean it is
accurate. However, if the information somehow enables
an individual to become a better person in the process,
it is probably worthwhile.

Primarily, the Akashic Records of the past provide individuals with a framework of potentials and probabilities in the present. That framework exists for everyone.
An individual doesn't need to be open to the possibility
of reincarnation for the records to impact his or her life,
relationships, thoughts, and activities. All individuals
constantly draw toward themselves the memory of their
previous activities, perfectly stored in the Akashic
Records database.

When dealing with the past, from Edgar Cayce's perspective, it wasn't so important who an individual had
once been; what was important was who an individual

was in the process of becoming in the present. The past merely provides a framework of data with which to work—what an individual does with that data becomes a matter of free will and a portion of the records for the rest of all time.

Past-Life Imaginative Reverie

Note: A reverie is best done with another person (reading the reverie like a script), or with oneself first narrating the reverie on a tape and then playing it back in order to experience the exercise. Although any historical period in history can be chosen, this particular reverie explores ancient Egypt. Reveries are generally narrated at about one-third the normal rate of speech.

NARRATION:

Get comfortable in your chair (or on a couch) and close your eyes. Take a deep breath, and tell yourself to relax. Take another deep breath—breathing in relaxation and calm, and slowly breathing out any tension or stress. Take another deep breath and relax.

Become comfortable and relaxed and begin focusing your attention on your breathing. Let your awareness begin to notice how cool the air feels as you inhale and how warm it feels as you breathe out. After a few moments, breathe in relaxation all the way down to your toes . . . breathe out any tension.

Breathe in relaxation to your feet and ankles . . . breathing out any tension. Breathe in relaxation to your legs and knees . . . breathe out any tension. Breathe in relaxation to your hips and buttocks . . . breathe out any tension. Next, relaxation to your stomach and back . . . breathe out any tension. Breathe in relaxation to your chest and shoulders . . . breathe out any tension. Breathe in relaxation to your arms and hands . . . breathe out any tension. Relaxation to your neck and head . . . breathe out any tension.

Finally, breathe in relaxation to your forehead and eyes, and breathe out any tension.

Even a light feeling of relaxation will give you an experience. This is an experience you'd like to feel . . . You are relaxed . . . eager to explore, and eager to learn. You don't have to make any special effort. You are in a place of safety . . . simply relax.

I am going to count downward from ten to one, and as I count—with every descending number—feel yourself becoming more and more relaxed. You will enter your own state of natural relaxation . . . completely relaxed . . . and completely aware of your mind, which is very much at peace . . .

Ten . . . nine . . . eight . . . seven . . . six . . . five . . . four . . . three . . . two . . . one . . .

You are now in a state of relaxation . . . completely aware of the activities of your mind . . . and aware of the sound of my voice.

You are going to let your mind wander back in time . . . to a safe place, before the present . . . You are going to learn about your past in Egypt . . . Totally relaxed . . . and detached, you will observe the best experience you lived in Egypt of long ago . . . You'll be able to see it clearly in your imagination with a feeling of total safety and security. Relax into your imagination and let yourself feel totally at peace. With your imagination, find yourself in Egypt of long ago . . . totally relaxed and totally in control. I want you to begin to imagine your *best* experience there . . .

Take a deep breath and feel comfortable. In your imagination, I want you to see yourself standing before the Great Pyramid of Gizeh . . . Slowly, ever so slowly, the magnificent structure coming into focus . . . and towering before you. With greater and greater clarity the Great Pyramid stands before you, majestic, soaring above the desert plains. You see the Pyramid as it was . . . in all its glory . . . as it appeared the very first time you saw it in this long ago past . . .

As you stand before the Great Pyramid, mentally look down at your feet . . . notice what you are wearing . . . or are they bare? Without analyzing, just look at your feet and mentally record what you sense or feel. What does it feel like to be who you are . . . standing before this magnificent emblem of Egypt? You might wish to say it to yourself, internally and quiet. [pause 5 seconds]

Look at the ground . . . what does it look like? Do you see grass . . . or soil . . . or desert sand? [pause for 5 seconds]

And now, continue to look slowly at your body. What are you wearing . . . ? Feel the texture . . . is it familiar, or some kind of unusual fabric? What colors do you have on? For a moment, look over your entire body and take into your mind the clothes you are wearing . . . [pause 5 seconds]

Are you a grownup, or a child . . . ? Are you a male or a female?

Do you have any jewelry? Is there anything on your head, or anything you may be holding in your hands . . . ? Focus on whatever appears to be in the clearest, sharpest focus. Make a mental note of who you are . . . and what you seem to be doing . . . [pause]

Now, in your mind's eye, slowly look around at the Gizeh plateau. Look around at the scenery. Feel the warmth of the sun upon your face . . . Feel the mood of this place . . . Make a mental note of what you see and feel. Are there trees, or just stretches and stretches of sand . . . ? Do you see other buildings or structures? Can you see the Sphinx . . . ? Make a mental note of your deepest feelings so that you can recall these things later. What does it feel like to be alive during these glorious days of Egypt . . . ? [pause]

Are there bushes . . . animals . . . people around you? If you have difficulty seeing, simply try to hear . . . or feel this place. Let the memories come forward as a present image . . .

This is your opportunity to experience this Egypt of the past. It is a time to think of things once thought . . . things once felt . . . and things once heard from your own past . . . For a moment, listen to the sounds of this glorious place, and make a mental note of what it is you hear . . . [pause]

And now, you may look around for other people. Look for a time when you're near other people. Make a mental note of who they are and what they look like . . . Perhaps there is someone very special . . . someone with whom you have a close bond. Perhaps it is a child or an adult . . . but it is someone very special. Someone who has great meaning to you . . . Make note of your feelings . . . if you listen quietly, you may even hear their names being spoken . . . [pause]

And now, if you listen very closely, you may hear your own name being spoken by a friend or a child, or maybe it's just someone calling out to you . . . What do they call you . . . ? What do you do in this Egypt of long ago . . . ? [pause]

You may wish to remember what the food was like. Can you remember a time when you were eating . . . ? Can you feel what it's like to taste something . . . ? Can you smell the food? Make a mental note for yourself of the meal . . . [pause]

Now, let's move to another episode. I'm going to count

backward from three, and when I reach one you will find yourself in a scene from your childhood in this Egyptian lifetime. Okay, three . . . two . . . one . . .

Do you see yourself . . . ? Are you playing . . . ? Getting into mischief . . . ? Lying upon the ground . . . ? Sitting in the lap of someone who loves you . . . ?

Look around at where you are. What's going on . . . ? Look at what you're wearing . . . Can you hear what the other people are saying . . . ? Take it all in. [pause]

I'm going to let you go to another period in your life. An important event when you're older. It may be a time that had important meaning to you; perhaps a major event in your life . . . I'm going to count back from three and you'll be there. Three . . . two . . . one . . . Focus on what is happening, and make a mental note to remember . . . [pause] Are people talking . . . ? What are they saying . . . ? Are you talking . . . ? Listen to the sounds of this place . . . what are you feeling . . . ? Take it all in. [pause]

Now, if you can, try to imagine what your purpose was in this Egypt of long ago . . . Was anything left uncompleted . . . ? [pause] See if you can look at this life in Egypt all at once. See all your life events tied together so that you can see the lifetime as a whole. Now, imagine all of the events of your *current* life right now in the twentieth century. See the two lives standing side by side: the one you are living now and the one from Egypt. Do you see any similarities . . . ? Do you see any patterns that repeated . . . ? Do you see any people whom you know now that you knew then . . . ? Look at all the similarities and patterns that connect these lives together . . . [pause]

Take a final look at your surroundings in this long ago past. Look into the eyes of the people you have seen . . . Let love flow from yourself into *everyone* from that long ago past. And as you send them love, bless them . . . and let them and your Egyptian surroundings begin to fade. And as they fade, let them go . . . release them . . . Forgive anything that needs to be forgiven so that only love remains . . . Let this experience slowly fade into the past, so that only positive and objective memories remain . . .

And as you slowly begin coming back, traveling back through time, you can bring with you all that was positive and bright, and interesting, and important. Other information you may release or forget. Bring back only something holy or special—something precious—a gem of wisdom, but only what you want . . . You will retain in your conscious mind only that which is helpful, important, and beneficial . . . [pause]

Now, begin returning to the current level of your own mind. Bring back anything that may help you understand who you are *right now* in *this* time and *this* place. Come back to the years in this life . . . Plant your feet firmly in the present . . . Become who you are *right now.* Your subconscious mind always protects you . . . you will have brought back only that which is helpful . . .

I will count from one to five. When I reach five you can open your eyes, be wide awake, clear-headed, happy, refreshed, and feeling fine. I will begin to count now . . . One, coming back very slowly . . . Two, feeling refreshed . . . Three, feeling revitalized . . . Four, fully reoriented into the present . . . And five, open your eyes and feel wide awake and perfectly normal.

Please note: You may wish to make a record of your experience while it is still fresh in your mind.

Part Two:

The Present

~

"He's a comical old fellow," said Scrooge's nephew,
    "that's the truth; and not so pleasant as he might be.
    However, his offenses carry their own punishment,
    and I have nothing to say against him."
"I'm sure he is very rich, Fred," hinted Scrooge's niece.
    "At least you always tell *me* so."
"What of that, my dear?" said Scrooge's nephew. "His
    wealth is of no use to him. He doesn't do any good
    with it. He doesn't make himself comfortable with it.
    He hasn't the satisfaction of thinking–ha, ha, ha!–
    that he is ever going to benefit us with it."
"I have no patience with him," observed Scrooge's
    niece. Scrooge's niece's sisters, and all the other
    ladies, expressed the same opinion.
"Oh, I have!" said Scrooge's nephew. "I am sorry for him:
    I couldn't be angry with him if I tried. Who suffers by
    his ill whims? Himself, always . . . "

Charles Dickens's A Christmas Carol

4

The Akashic Records as an Indicator of the Present

⁂

Yes, we have the entity, the soul-mind, and the mental and
material mind of the entity now known as [256], with those
experiences of the soul in the earthly sojourns with the devel-
opments and the environments in the present, and that which
has been builded by the entity as to what the entity has done
respecting that which has builded into what is now present in
the earth.

256-5

*I*magine every morning when you awakened that
you were presented with a computer-generated listing
of each person, task, and experience which would be

most beneficial for you to encounter as a part of your day. What if each of these experiences had been selected by an omniscient database which had your best interests at heart? Imagine, as well, that each of these experiences had the potential to assist you in not only overcoming all of your shortcomings and becoming the very best person you could be, but also in fulfilling your personal mission in life. Would you want to look at the list?

According to Edgar Cayce, the Akashic Records constantly provide us with the very experiences and relationships that we need at the present time. Whether or not we face those experiences and people (who may just as readily appear to be "positive" as they do "negative") in the best possible manner becomes a matter of free will. Every choice, thought, and decision we make in the present has an effect upon the substance of the next series of potentials and probabilities we draw toward us. In the language of the readings, "For ever, day by day, is there a choice to be made by each soul" (1538-1). One set of choices may lead to growth, transformation, and ultimately happiness, and the other may lead to further problems, frustrations, and personal difficulties. Although we may not be conscious of the fact that everything we are encountering in life can become meaningful and purposeful, the readings suggest that such potential is ever present.

For example, two people might face a similar circumstance—say the loss of a job—yet each person might deal with the situation in a very different manner. One might spend a great deal of time and energy becoming bitter and angry over what happened, and the other might see it as a wonderful opportunity to "start all over" and do something which has always been a desire. Although the situation is the same, each person's response is quite different. The way a person responds to a situation determines the next cycle, the next crossroads called into action. Thwarting simplicity, however, is the fact that each of us experiences multiple cycles at any given time. And each of these potential realities is created from the evolving storehouse of information contained within the Akashic Records.

Whenever he gave a reading, Cayce chose his information from the records with care. Not only were there particular lives which were having the greatest influence on the individual in the here and now, but there were urges and emotions that were both latent and manifested operating within the individual's consciousness at any given time—not all of which were positive. These urges could grow or diminish based on the individual's choices and resulting experiences. The Akashic Records act as a giant computer database, storing memories and patterns that can be drawn upon at any time.

Within these records, we possess positive and negative patterns of behavior. According to Cayce, these patterns are tapped and further developed by our present thought processes and activities. With free will, a soul can develop along the lines of either a saint or a monster. Since it is just as easy to pick up and continue to cultivate a negative pattern of behavior as a positive one, the readings frequently advised individuals to set an ideal—a purposeful, positive intent against which they could measure their potential thoughts and actions in the present. This method of weighing daily life against a spiritual ideal was called, "the most important experience of this or any individual entity . . . " (357-13).

In 1938 a secretary told Edgar Cayce that all her life she had recounted vivid memories of another life when she had died as a child at the age of five or six (1608-1). She wanted additional information on that experience. In a reading, Cayce stated that her memories were real and that she had died ten years prior to her present birth. However, she was advised not to dwell upon those memories—it was best to set the information aside. Her present life demanded her attention for there was much she could be doing if she directed her ideals and purposes in the proper channels.

What makes reincarnation important is that the past lays much of the groundwork for an individual's opportunities in the present. In the case of one woman who was a model and whose hands were billed as "the most photographed in the world," Cayce traced their extraordinary beauty to a life she had lived in a convent. Her hands were in such demand today that she had become famous among advertisers for featuring products such as hand lotion, nail polish, and jewelry. According to the reading, in the convent the woman had been assigned menial and distasteful work that the readings described as "unsightly." In spite of the unpleasantness, the woman had performed her tasks with such duty, love, patience, and service that eventually her selflessness had become manifested in the beauty of her hands (1286-1).

In the same way that talents were traced to the past, an individual's present-day challenges frequently found their roots in choices and decisions that had been made previously. For example, a forty-one-year-old woman (2329-1) came to Edgar Cayce for help in trying to understand and deal with a problem which was making her an emotional and physical wreck. She had been married for eighteen years to a wonderful man whom she described as loving and considerate; unfortunately he was impotent. Not knowing what else to do, the woman throughout their marriage had satisfied her sexual cravings with occasional liaisons with other men—a situation about which she felt extremely guilty.

Recently, an old suitor had entered into her life and

the two had gotten together. However, guilt—and the fact that the man was married—caused the woman to break off the affair. The man continued to pursue her, confusing her all the more. To make matters worse, the woman's doctor wanted her to begin taking estrogen for a health condition. The woman feared taking the hormone would increase her sexual tension. The emotional conflict between loving her husband and desperately wanting to resume the affair (about which she felt guilt to begin with) were taking a physical toll.

As usual, Cayce began the reading with, "Yes, we have the records here of that entity now known as or called [2329]." During the reading, Cayce confirmed that the present situation had developed in the past—in a lifetime that she and her husband had shared during the Crusades. At the time, her husband, to insure the woman's fidelity while he was away as a soldier, forced her to wear a chastity belt. Apparently he was away for a long time, and she eventually desired sexual companionship, but there was nothing she could do about the situation. As a result, she harbored deep hatred, anger, and resentment toward him, "determining to sometime, somewhere . . . 'get even.' " (2329-1) She was told that the present situation was her opportunity to overcome the resentment that had been built hundreds of years previously—the woman was simply meeting herself.

Rather than advising the woman which course to take about the affair, Cayce told her that she had to weigh the decision against her own feelings and beliefs. However, it was important for her to remember that anything done with the intent of helping another person would lead to growth and anything done solely for personal and selfish gratification could only lead to further difficulties.

It is important to point out that in spite of a person's

differing urges, tendencies, and subconscious memories of past lives, the readings always emphasized that how individuals dealt with their present life, their present relationships, and the choices and opportunities which confronted them was of the utmost importance. From Edgar Cayce's perspective, reincarnation was neither a belief system nor a philosophy; it was, instead, a factual process of personal development, eventually enabling each individual to reach soul maturity as a loving, creative, selfless being. For him, the present was what really mattered. It was not so important who an individual might have been in the past, but what she or he was doing in the present.

Throughout the forty-three years he gave readings, Edgar Cayce emphasized that the information he chose from the boundless supply of available data was intended to assist the individual in best meeting those challenges and opportunities which he or she now faced. On a number of occasions while putting himself into an altered state to give a reading, Cayce became conscious of journeying to a "hall of records" in some manner and meeting an old man surrounded by volumes of books. The old man would hand him the record of the individual with whom Cayce was working. While in this state of consciousness, Cayce would select from the record that information which would be most helpful and hopeful for the person at the present time. Oftentimes the readings tried to explain to individuals why they were being confronted with certain experiences and— without interfering with their free will—provide them with practical ways of dealing with whatever was occurring in their present life.

In December 1940, while giving a reading to a young woman, Cayce had an encounter with the old man with the books which seemed to emphasize the importance of this selectivity of information. Cayce recalled the experience as follows:

> It is the only time I've had the Keeper of Records to point out to me what I can read. Always before he has merely handed me the book but I didn't remember reading out of the book. Here he guided my reading of the book, and pointed with his finger at the passages I might read, and told me what parts to skip until later.
>
> Case 2390-2 Report File

On another occasion, in reading 2281-1, Cayce stated that he was being warned by the old man with the books to be "mindful" in selecting that information which would be most helpful and hopeful to the young woman who had requested the reading.

Once Cayce had accessed the Akashic Records, explored the effects of planetary influences, and discussed past lives, he would explain how these urges were impacting the present. Rather than some philosophical discourse, the advice was intended to be practical, helping individuals with all manner of difficulties: relationships, health concerns, personal pain, and even career direction.

For example, a young woman came to Edgar Cayce seeking vocational guidance (3342-1). She had changed jobs so many times that she doubted she had been with any of her previous employers for an entire year. Even from the Akashic Records the woman's confusion was apparent, for Cayce began with "Yes, we have the records here—what a muddle puddle, and yet what a beautiful, what a talented soul!"

Later, Cayce suggested that his desire was to provide the woman encouragement in discovering and utilizing her present talents. The reading stated that the woman would find greatest happiness in helping others and Cayce suggested working as a teacher with young women and girls. He also suggested that she excelled at helping those who were less fortunate and he recommended active service in the Red Cross. He pointed out that the woman had talent in art and music. She had a deep appreciation of spirituality and should teach Sunday school.

A number of the woman's characteristics were discussed and applauded: her depth of emotion, her gentleness, her graciousness, her sense of duty, her talent at showing others by example, her gift at bringing joy into her surroundings, and her ability to meet any problem that arose. Her abilities—especially with young ladies—were "far beyond the ordinary," and she was encouraged to apply herself. When the woman asked, "Any other advice?" Cayce replied, "Why tell beauty to be beautiful? Just keep sweet. We are through."

At the time of the reading, the woman commented that the information she received "certainly expresses my most inmost desires and aspirations." She also stated that she had been drawn to working with girls and should have done it sooner, but would follow through on his advice. In 1957, twelve years after Edgar Cayce had died, the woman submitted a follow-up report. She had done a great deal of work with girls and was currently employed at Boston University in charge of a dormitory for 150 young women! She continued Red Cross work and had been active in disaster work. She was also involved in Girl Scouts and loved camping. She had been active in her Methodist church, where she played piano and sang in the choir. She was no longer confused about her life.

In another instance, a woman who had spent years in

her position as a telegraph operator (338) was told that she possessed innate artistic talents which should and could be greatly utilized in the present. Although she had no artistic background, she attended art school because of the reading. Her instructor was pleased with her talent, noting her "unusual abilities." After a year of study, she become a popular commercial artist and later told Mr. Cayce that she made more money in one month than she had made in a year as a telegraph operator.

A thirty-three-year-old man who worked in a bank wrote Mr. Cayce in August 1938 for insights into how his talents could best be channeled to benefit others. Although his job was satisfactory, he wondered if there wasn't something more fulfilling he could do. An avid amateur radio enthusiast, he facilitated ongoing communications among the United States, the Far East, Peru, and Western Australia. In the reading, Cayce traced the man's ability with accounting to a prior lifetime in which he had served others by assisting them in keeping personal records and accounts of their goods and supplies. The reading confirmed the man's interest in communications and stated it was a talent he had developed in ancient Persia, relaying messages between various lands and trading outposts. He had also tapped this same aptitude for communications in later lives in Greece and Spain, developing his ability until it was his first love. Cayce stated that the man's position in the bank was the outgrowth of circumstance and that he would find the greatest degree of personal fulfillment in "those abilities in communications" (1681-1).

In 1965 the gentleman once again came in contact with Edgar Cayce's Association and wrote to report how accurately the reading had described him:

I had really forgotten much of the data in my life

reading and was amazed to find how closely the last few years have followed the general direction of communication which it mentions. In addition to my amateur radio interest—now centered entirely in communication between Eye-Banks, to keep them informed as to need for and availability of corneal transplant material, it has been a duty and pleasure to lecture to several hundred groups on the drug industry, socialized medicine, etc.

Case 1681-1 Report File

Not everyone who received a reading was able to follow the advice Cayce prescribed. Due in part to his wife's encouragement, in 1938 a forty-year-old man (1538-1) procured a reading about the type of work he should pursue. With the exception of a brief stint in the army, his wife stated that her husband had "drifted from one position to another." In addition to his lack of regular work, he frequently gambled, dallied in brief liaisons with other women, and drank a great deal. He was extremely handsome and seemed to have an ability to quickly make friends. However, he was not a good judge of character and he had been fired from a regular job in 1935 apparently for taking money from his office in order to pay off "friends" who were bookies.

Twice his wife had confronted him about their financial strain and his gambling and insisted that something be done about the situation. Both times he had disappeared, taken to drink, and ended up in the veteran's hospital. His wife stated on both occasions she had felt so sorry for him that she had taken him back. Together, they hoped a reading would help solve their problems. Because of the couple's financial situation and their inability to pay for a reading, a friend of Mr. Cayce's had given it to them as a gift.

After acquiring the records, Cayce stated that Mr. [1538] was extremely sensitive to people and to surroundings. It was also pointed out that he was too easily influenced and manipulated by others, a trait which, unless overcome, would eventually lead to additional "discouragements, disturbing forces and influences in the experience in this sojourn." (1538-1) Because the man had never established a conscious ideal or motivation for his life, he was a "drifter." Cayce warned that unless an ideal was chosen, Mr. [1538] would never be at peace with himself.

The reading advised the man to stop blaming others for his predicament. He had definite strengths which could be utilized in the present, but instead Mr. [1538] had too often fallen into his old weaknesses. In addition to discussing his internal conflict and warring emotions, Cayce suggested that he had an innate ability to do work in a commissary or to even serve as a shipping clerk. In fact, the reading stated that he had been commander of the commissary around (what is now) Washington, D.C., during the American Revolution. When [1538] asked about the possibility of returning to government service, Cayce suggested that he was especially suited for the army or the supply depot and would probably find work in Quantico or Yorktown, Virginia.

Unfortunately, [1538] never followed through on his reading. Years later his ex-wife reported that he had gone so far as to schedule an interview with the army but "when the time came to keep it he lost his courage and nerve and didn't keep the appointment." They eventually divorced, and the husband said that his wife had "let *him* down." Mr. [1538] would eventually marry again, separate, and divorce after two years. Later, he would marry the same woman a second time and finally separate. In time he would find work in shipbuilding and dry dock. He died in 1976 at the age of 80. His first wife stated that on the various occasions she had seen him, there were times when he did look good but others when "he looked as though he was very unhappy." In all likelihood, Mr. [1538] never made peace with himself.

Nowhere did Cayce place a greater emphasis on the importance of free will and decision making than he did to parents in the rearing and directing of their children during the formative years. In one of the most notable examples, the parents of an eleven-year-old boy were told that the records for the child could be interpreted "either in a very optimistic or a very pessimistic vein" (3633-1). Cayce stated that the child was inclined to "think more highly of himself than he ought to think" and that the boy's greatest talents lay in music, writing, or poetry. A budding genius, the child could use his abilities to bring joy to others or he could use them for his own selfishness—a tendency which the soul had previously followed. The young man was inclined to "disregard others altogether . . . just so self has its own way."

Cayce stated in the reading, "There are unlimited abilities. How will they be directed by the entity? How well may others cause the entity to be aware of such activities? These should be the questions in self." The child's rearing was extremely important because his talents, his weaknesses, and his genius were so developed that they would give him the opportunity to become "either a Beethoven or a Whittier or a Jesse James . . . " Seven years later, the boy shot and wounded his father and his grandmother. He was later sent to a state hospital, treated for schizophrenia, and would die two weeks following his thirty-first birthday.

One of the underlying principles which Cayce gleaned from the Akashic Records was the importance of personal responsibility in shaping the course of our lives and the condition of the world around us. Simply stated, we have an effect upon every soul we encounter, and we have an integral role in creating our lives, our experiences, our relationships, even world events. In Cayce's terminology, our life is not destined; instead, we are active "cocreators" in its unfoldment.

The focus of Cayce's work was never upon himself or his psychic prowess; instead, his desire was to provide individuals with practical information and guidance which could assist them in dealing with their life challenges and decisions. In addition to providing information which was most relevant to an individual in her or his current life experience, Cayce frequently discussed the reality of an ever-present, loving God who was always mindful of His creation. Although not generally known, in addition to his psychic work, Cayce spent much of his time corresponding with those individuals who had asked for his help. Just as in the readings, the advice he gave suggested that individuals were very much involved in a cocreative process of their unfolding lives.

In 1937 a thirty-year-old woman, who had received a reading, wrote Edgar Cayce to tell him of her struggle with depression and lethargy. She described her state of mind as follows:

> . . . since about the middle of November I have been struggling through a "Slough of Despond." Why, I don't exactly know, but suspect that it is due to a great extent to the fact that I'm really very unhappy inside—unhappy because I am dissatisfied with my life and myself—not accomplishing anything worthwhile and apparently lacking in that subtle spark which drives people on to accomplish great things. Unhappy, too, because I am lonely . . . Though I want to work and keep busy, I am tired of

struggling as so many of us do for mere existence, becoming so wearied in mind, body and spirit, in the process, that there's nothing left to give to God and our fellow beings. My health has never been particularly good either and may be partly responsible for my despondency. I seem to be always feeling below par . . .

A few days later—January 15, 1937, Cayce wrote and tried to counsel her about the impact her thoughts were having upon her life. Long before the awareness of such terms as "the power of positive thinking" or "prosperity thinking" or the constructive nature of personal affirmations, the Cayce readings emphasized that "mind is the builder" and that each individual is constantly involved in the creation of underlying attitudes and emotions. His advice was as follows:

. . . Thanks for yours of the 12th. I appreciate your taking time to write. I think I can fully appreciate your feelings, for I, too, have periods when there seems to be nothing that can or will come right, getting nowhere and the outlook anything but promising. It is indeed one thing to know, and quite another thing to put into daily practice, that we do know. But there is where wisdom comes in, for, will we but realize that the power to choose, the power to exercise wisdom is within our own minds, we will accomplish much more by simply meditating, or as the Good Book says, meet God in the temple of our own bodies. He has promised to do so, and always keeps that promise; not to something outside ourselves but within, and listen to the still, small voice within. For, we remember even the sages of old, whether those given us in the Scripture, or in other writings, it is always the same.

And let that prayer or meditation be something like this, though always put it in your own words: "I am the child of the Infinite Life, that flows within me, has built for me a perfect temple to live in. When I live and move and have my being in it, with Faith and Love, it guides me, protects me and watches over me, day and night. So, I am renewed each day, filled with Health, Wealth, Love, Freedom, Peace of mind, Serenity of Soul. And now I thank Thee, Father, and rest in Peace for all is Well." Something like that in your own words not merely said each night and morning, but said in such manner that you feel His Presence, will change your health, and your outlook on life. Won't you give it a try?

Case 1286-1 Report File

In a similar manner, the reading for a fifty-three-year-old wife and mother stated that many of her problems were due to her fears, her self-criticism, and her constant worry. Cayce told her:

How, ye ask, is this applicable in the experience of this entity now known as or called [793]? That will, that fear of what may become a part of the experience is such in the experience of the entity that so oft does it find and has it found this very condition PREVENTING self from enjoying even its greater joys. For so oft is the attitude, "Yes—but tomorrow is a change. Yes—but can that be true for me? Yes—but I have not accomplished that which is my ideal. Yes—but I have fallen short of that as I would do. Yes—but they will soon be grown, thinking their own thoughts, going their own ways."

And the entity has let so much of this INTERFERE

with and prevent the real joy of the beauties, the
joys, the wonderful grace that has ever been and is
so near to each soul that seeks to know His face.

793-2

Too often, when individuals speak about their personal experiences, world events, changing times, or their
"karma," they discuss these things from a fatalistic view-
point: *All these things are happening to me, and there is
nothing I can do about it.* In other words, any awareness
one might have regarding personal responsibility and
cocreation is easily forgotten. Frequently, individuals in
contemporary society have grown accustomed to responding to life as a victim. One of the readings puts a
humorous twist on this idea of victimization:

> Q. Is there likelihood of bad health in March?
> A. If you are looking for it you can have it in Feb-
> ruary! If you want to skip March, skip it—you'll have
> it in June! If you want to skip June, don't have it at all
> this year!

3564-1

Today, we often seem to avoid personal responsibility
for the events and circumstances of our lives: *I am no
longer responsible for the things that happen to me. The
condition of my life is because of what other people have
done to me. It's because of my karma. Someone did something to me, and therefore I need to sue them.* We may
blame our parents, our upbringing, our neighbors, our
society, even our past lives for our present situation.

In July 1936, a twenty-two-year-old man (1233-1) simply wanted to know from which side of his family he had
inherited most of his traits. He was told, "You have inherited most from yourself, not from family. The family

is only a river through which it (the entity, soul) flows!" From the readings' perspective, life is a continuous experience and we are constantly meeting ourselves.

During the course of one reading, a housewife was told about her present talents and abilities: being a good listener, having the capacity to correlate and understand Eastern and Western thought, and her ability to reason with others. She was also interested in pursuing a line of work with a very successful businessman to whom she was drawn. Her reading stated that together they had once ruled a vast empire and in the present could accomplish a great deal if her ideals and purposes were used correctly. She submitted a list of people who had been important in her life—all of whom, Cayce confirmed, had been with her in the past. In addition to discussing relevant past lives and the influence these individuals were having in the present, he provided insights into what the woman had been trying to learn in each situation. Immediately after receiving the reading, the woman responded, "So amazing! So perfectly true as to all those relationships; just exactly the conditions that exist today between us!" (Case 1554-3 Report File)

Our relationships with one another are an ongoing process, from which we can learn a great deal about ourselves. We never meet anyone by chance. Instead, souls are drawn together again and again for possible personal soul development—a development, ultimately, which will assist each individual in becoming a fit companion with the Creator. Frequently, when individuals asked how to deal with challenging personalities in their lives, they were told to merely minimize the faults of others and magnify their virtues. Although this might sound simplistic, in reading 2791-1, Cayce stated that he used this same principle when selecting information about an individual from her or his own Akashic Record.

Throughout the many years of his work, Cayce seemed uniquely adept at contacting the Akashic Records and providing any information imaginable. Whether personal insights, historical data, or material related to the collective lessons and evolving futures of world nations, there appeared to be no limit to his talent for accessing the universe's immense database. However, contained within the thousands of readings on file, there are a few occasions when Edgar Cayce either would not or could not tap into the Akashic Records and provide the questioner with the information he or she sought.

For example, although it was attempted, Cayce could not give the reading which had been scheduled for the morning of June 10, 1933 (case 355) [note: the reading was obtained on 6/13/33]. Later, in one of the Work Readings (those readings which dealt with Cayce's abilities and the work of his Association), he was asked about why he had been unable to provide the information when originally requested. In response to the question, Cayce stated that the process of giving a reading was a very fine and delicate procedure. There were a number of factors which would make contacting the records impossible by hindering, repelling, or blocking his subconscious mind. Those factors included the unwillingness of Edgar Cayce's physical body to submit to the suggestion of entering into the unconscious state or the state of his physical health. However, other factors included the mental thoughts of those individuals in the room if they were "not in accord with the type, class or character of information sought at that particular time" (254-67). Because of the sensitivity of the process, as well as the difficulty of interpreting the records themselves, anyone present for a reading had to be unified in her or his desire to be of help to the questioner. It was the absence of this factor, the reading explained, which had blunted

Cayce's ability "to reach that position, that plane, that sphere, from which the record was being sought," preventing him from giving [355]'s reading in the first place.

On other occasions, Edgar Cayce was able to access the Akashic Records and give an entire reading, but he seemed unable to provide answers to a specific question. In those instances, he might respond with "that cannot be given from here" or "we do not have the information." In those cases when the readings stated that the information could not be given, one reason was because a response might interfere with the individual's use of his or her own free will in the experience. One case is that of Mrs. [1523], when the readings refused to reveal to her that her ex-husband was about to reenter her life and she would be torn between him and her second husband. The reading withheld this information with the rationale that "To give as to what such would be, would not be in keeping with the entity's using self's OWN will, self's own choice or judgment" (1523-11).

Information sometimes could not be given because there were too many conditional factors involved. One young woman could not be told how long before there would be improvements in her medical condition because those attending her were responsible for "continued changes" in the quantity and caliber of the medicine she was receiving (case 543-10).

In those cases when the readings stated, "We do not have the information," oftentimes the failure to answer a specific question appears to be connected to the original suggestion Cayce received when he entered into the unconscious state. For example, at the end of reading 540-4 a housewife asked for information about her past association with her daughter. Cayce said that he did not have the information from the Akashic Records. He told her that the only information he had available was material which detailed her past-life experience as a woman named Naomi in Palestine during the time of Jesus. Interestingly, that information was exactly what had been asked for when the original suggestion had been given. Apparently, the old man with the books had given Cayce's subconscious mind just what he had requested.

Once, while providing further information about the Akashic Records—"the records . . . upon time and space"—their interpretation, and their location, Cayce stated:

> As to the place of records—this is a place, yet it is everywhere. It, the information, to be individualized, must come from some source into some form to be interpreted in the experience of the seeker . . .
>
> Then, the record is thine. How, then—ye ask—may this individual ye call Edgar Cayce interpret same? How do I know such is a correct interpretation? From whence is same read? With what is there the interpreting of happenings physical, of associations with material purposes and desires, under those environs when quite a different manner or language was used in interpreting the associations and activities? Whence cometh such a knowledge to one individual, as to interpret the records of another through varied spheres of activity or experience?
>
> Only as a gift of Him who has given, "If ye keep my ways, I will love thee, will abide with thee, and bring to thy remembrance ALL things from the foundation of the world."
>
> Then, while the source may be entirely capable of bringing a full or complete knowledge, the answers must ever be according to the law just given—within thine own self.
>
> 2072-8

In reading 254-67, Cayce said that the Akashic Records could be read by a psychic, but they could also be deduced by the individual who had written the record to begin with. Asked how this was possible, the reading confirmed that the records were everywhere and were manifested through one's consciousness by means of the five senses. In other words, our patterns and our abilities become evident through what we say, what we write, what we choose to see, and what we choose to hear. According to Cayce, each of these things, as well as our thoughts, are affected by the "shadows" of what is written upon the records themselves. Clarity of obtaining specific information is dependent upon why the information is being sought in the first place.

Another individual (2498-1) was told that much of the information contained within the Akashic Records was written in symbolic form and required interpretation. This premise was further explored in a 1933 reading which discussed whether or not the Akashic Records contained real books.

While giving the reading, Edgar Cayce saw himself traveling through water in a bubble and arriving at the place where he always got his information. It was there that he met the old man with the books. As to whether or not the books were "real," Cayce stated that the subconscious would utilize whatever symbols were required to bring to mental consciousness the fact that information was being obtained from one realm and being communicated to another. He went on to state that if an individual required the images of fields or flowers or birds in order to communicate to the mental mind the fact that information was being obtained from beyond the material plane, that is exactly what the individual would see. Therefore, because much of the world associated books with enlightenment, then many individuals might associate the Akashic Records with *real* books (254-68).

Throughout history, much of the information contained within the Akashic Records related to patterns of human behavior and experience has been symbolized in art, literature, Scripture, fairy tale, and legend. Cayce stated that these stories frequently paralleled the origin, development, and destiny of humankind. Sometimes they have managed to explore universal truths or archetypes in such a way as to resonate to individuals at a soul level, becoming classics in the process.

For example, the story of the soul is one in which the soul was with the Creator in the beginning. With our own free will, we have been choosing experiences that have enabled us to develop our own sense of individuality. At the same time, however, we are constantly searching to regain our true relationship with God. That relationship is our destiny. Simply stated, we were with the Creator in the beginning, we went astray, and ultimately we will return to our true home. This pattern—encapsulating our collective past, present, and future—is stored within the database of the Akashic Records. However, that very same theme is related to us in such stories as the Parable of the Prodigal Son, Dorothy's journey in *The Wizard of Oz*, as well as the journeys of Christian, Bilbo, and Pinocchio in *Pilgrim's Progress*, *The Hobbit*, and the *Adventures of Pinocchio*, respectively. The closer a story, a character, or a situation can come to symbolizing a valid universal archetype stored in the Akashic Records, the more it captures human imagination for all time and becomes mythic.

According to Edgar Cayce, the Akashic Records constantly provide individuals with exactly those experiences and relationships they need at a particular time in order to learn whatever lesson is necessary for the soul's growth and development. Each of us contains many urges, patterns, and conflicting emotions that must be resolved in the soul's educational process of discovering "who am I?" Whether or not these lessons are learned in the present becomes a matter of free choice, but if they are not learned, they will simply be presented again and again in various ways until they are mastered.

From the readings' perspective, the earth is literally a "cause and effect" classroom in which each individual constantly has the opportunity to meet self and apply spiritual principles in the material world. Although this process of meeting self is not an easy one, it will be less traumatic if individuals set a spiritual intent (or ideal) for their lives. In a very real sense, the universe's computer system is responsible for our best interests. The records are designed to enable all individuals to discover their true identity, their relationship with God, and their connection with one another. And, as if to make this process all the more feasible, Cayce reminded us, "the records are everywhere."

5

Case Histories

(Note: Actual names have been changed in order to maintain confidentiality.)

Throughout the years he gave readings, Edgar Cayce suggested that individuals were repeatedly brought together, continuing relationships exactly where they had left off in the past. Because of our sojourns through time and space, we are essentially archaeological digs, containing layers of past lives, personal urges, and patterns which eventually find their way to the surface.

This attraction to one another was clearly evident among Cayce's contemporaries and those individuals most connected to his work. One 1928 reading (254-47) suggested that there were so many people being drawn back together that it would be possible to calculate their responses to one another in the present based upon the experiences they had encountered in the past. The reading suggested that such a comparison would be an interesting undertaking.

Perhaps with that in mind, the following year members of the Association began a Historical Committee, responsible for correlating the past-life relationships of various members of the Association and the impact those influences were having upon the present. Although not long in duration, the work proved fascinating and demonstrated not only the effects of the past but also the importance of free will in enabling some individuals to learn to accept and to deal with one another.

One of the individuals most integrally connected with Cayce's work was Stephen Levine [900]. By most accounts, Stephen was a financial and intellectual genius. By the time he had turned thirty, he had achieved great financial success and held a seat on the New York Stock Exchange. Self-certain, he was among the few individuals of Cayce's contemporaries who could easily understand some of the most complicated concepts explored in the readings. Due to his wealth and his own great interest in Cayce's work, he became the principal financial backer of the Association. He was also extremely interested in higher education and desired to create a university which would bring together the greatest minds of the world.

Robert Mitchell [165] was a successful businessman and manufacturer, deeply interested in the Cayce work as it related to health and education. He had once written that "Education is a method of living—strengthened by experience—broadened by learning—governed by independent and judicial thinking." He believed, "If all the world understood what it means to be educated, and how impossible is real progress without education . . .

most of our problems would disappear." He possessed the innate talents of a diplomat and a conqueror. It was the former he needed to draw upon in his interactions with Stephen Levine, for he felt that the young man had too much control of Cayce's Association. Although their joint interest in Cayce's work had brought them together, and their support of education should have cemented a friendship, the relationship between the two was more cautionary than friendly. At fifty years old, Robert Mitchell rightly believed he had more wisdom and experience in life than a thirty-four-year-old stockbroker—even though he did not have as much money.

In an effort to help the two men in their present relationship, the Historical Committee put together an overview of their past-life connections. The committee's premise was that "to understand a condition is to become master of it." Briefly, the information which the readings had gleaned from the Akashic Records is as follows:

In ancient Egypt, Stephen Levine was a talented scribe and a native Egyptian whose homeland had been conquered by an invading king from the north. In the present, that king would become Robert Mitchell. Although the new king created a new government and enacted many laws which would eventually benefit the Egyptian empire, he was still a "foreigner." In time, the scribe's talents would be brought to the government's attention and he would be given a responsible position representing native Egyptians. He became the primary communications link between the king and the native people. Although he had been among the oppressed natives, he had fulfilled his position with such an attitude of helpfulness that in the present it was Stephen who had been given control over others. In the words of the Historical Committee:

Always there was the feeling of suppression since you were a native and the ruler was an outsider but you worked and cooperated with each and every one in building up your country and in giving much to the peoples in understanding the moral, civil, and spiritual truths. Today for the development you made in that period and in others you have been chosen as the one to head up this WORK and have the ability to give to mankind a better understanding of their relation to their Creator. You worked then under great difficulties and gained. This time the power to retard or advance the work lies in your hands . . .

Case 900-275 Report File

Quite naturally, this situation created antagonistic feelings between the two men. Because Robert Mitchell had formerly been in control, he frequently seemed to question the decisions made by an individual who was not only younger and more inexperienced, but who had also once been his subordinate. Conversely, Stephen no longer felt the need to be oppressed and seemed quick to anger whenever it appeared as though Robert Mitchell was questioning him. Also, deep within himself, Stephen couldn't seem to overcome the feeling that [165] had simply returned to conquer. Conversely, Robert couldn't seem to overcome the feeling that [900] really didn't like him.

There had been another lasting connection between the two in Palestine. At one time, during the rebuilding of the walls of Jerusalem, Robert Mitchell (as an armorbearer) had fought against the return of the "chosen people." One of the enemies he had battled against (and lost) was [900], who was attempting to regain his homeland. It was this experience and the one in Egypt which created innate feelings of antagonism.

Regardless of where these feelings originated, the Historical Committee pointed out that both men had much to offer the Cayce work. In addition to his financial backing, Stephen Levine's quick mind enabled him to be not only a student, but also a teacher of the readings' philosophy. Robert Mitchell, on the other hand, had the ability to motivate and energize people on behalf of a cause. It was also evident that, with his business background and his years of experience, he could provide much advice and counsel for Cayce's young Association. The two men were encouraged to cooperate, learn from one another, and to keep in mind that—regardless of past experiences—they were now on the same side. The Historical Committee added, "Certainly neither of you must leave a stone unturned to try to cooperate with the other. It is a hard job. Yes. But the progress of the human soul means one hard job after another."

In spite of the advice, the two never resolved the difficulty in their relationship. With the stock market crash and financial challenges for both men, working together did not seem of great importance. In time Stephen would become concerned that other individuals were using him for his money and he withdrew himself and his financial support from the Association. Robert remained involved in the Association and was not upset by the young man's departure. In fact, he wrote Edgar Cayce telling him that with [900]'s departure perhaps those remaining with the work could now carry on more "sanely and cheerfully and energetically and prayerfully." Their opportunity to work together had failed. Robert Mitchell would die in 1940 and Stephen Levine would die more than ten years later. Since the relationship remained unresolved, from the readings' perspective, a time shall come when the Akashic Records will again draw the two together.

A more successful outcome was evident in the case of two college students, Andy Evans [341] and Jim McMahon [849] whose past-life difficulties with each other began during the very same period in ancient Egypt.

Interested in the Cayce work, Andy had been warned that at college he would come in contact with challenges that he needed to address. Apparently he was destined to encounter teachers and classmates with whom he had been associated previously. A number of individuals would be favorably drawn to him, but there would be obvious antagonism with others. In fact, some of these challenges would prove quite trying and he was encouraged to show himself "master of the situation." The reading suggested that since he was forewarned, he could make himself forearmed.

It was not long before Andy met one of the greatest challenges in his life in the personality of Jim McMahon. Assigned as roommates at college, each in a very short time found delight in causing difficulty for the other. Andy was from the South and Jim was from the Northeast—a "damn Yankee," Andy would later recall. From the very first (at least from Andy's perspective) Jim came across as superior, making Andy feel as though he were from some hick, small town.

Shortly after arrival at school, Andy wrote to his parents that the reading had been correct. There were a number of people he got along with and they got along with him; however, he found others "perplexing" and extremely difficult for him to deal with.

Both young men were attracted to philosophy, theology, and debate. Jim had been raised Catholic and Andy's parents were interested in reincarnation. Each found great joy in belittling the other's upbringing and beliefs. In time their relationship evolved to the point of pranks—

hiding each other's belongings—and frequent disagree-
ments. Sometimes, late at night, they'd get into argu-
ments so volatile that Jim would throw his mattress into
the hallway to sleep. In spite of the fact that they had to
room together, the anger between the two of them included fistfights and black eyes. Within a few months'
time, their college rivalry became an all-out "feud,"
known to others in the dormitory.

Eventually it was learned that Jim was more open to
the philosophy of reincarnation than he had admitted.
His openness led to a life reading from Mr. Cayce. Andy
also had a life reading. It was the readings which traced
the antagonism between the two throughout several periods in history.

In ancient Egypt, the two had frequently rebelled
against each other. Possessing different ideologies, Jim
managed to make himself a thorn in Andy's side. In time,
Andy would arrange to have Jim killed in a battle. During
the Crusades the two fought each other in hand-to-hand
combat. Andy's medieval counterpart was a Christian;
Jim was a Moslem. In one battle, Jim cut Andy with a
sword between his thumb and index finger. Years later,
Andy would recall, "when we argued, the scar would re-
appear there. It was weird—just a reminder." Finally,
they had been rivals in an English monastery, finding frequent opportunities to argue, disagree, and debate. It
seemed as though their college encounter was their
fourth experience of rivalry.

Both young men were challenged to attempt to overcome the centuries of antagonism. Andy was reminded
to keep to his ideals and purposes. He was told that he
would find great strength if the two tried to work together. It also became clear that they had a choice. They
could work on their relationship with each other or they
could separate and go in their own directions. The two

were encouraged to do the former.

Andy and Jim decided to work together. They spoke frequently about their difficulties, their feelings, and their lives in general. Each hoped that these conversations would "lead to a newer and better understanding between us." Although it was not always easy, they were determined to get along. They found that each had talents and abilities that were admired by the other. Through perseverance, Andy and Jim built a mutually agreeable friendship. They graduated from the university in June of 1930.

Years later, Andy would recall, "[Jim] and I worked through one of the most difficult pieces of karma that I have ever seen and we became friends at a level well beyond the average friendship." The two remained friends the rest of their lives. Jim found a measure of success as a writer. Andy became a businessman and lecturer.

While still a young man, Jim became ill with crippling arthritis. Andy opened his home and arranged to have Jim live with his family because the weather was more conducive to Jim's recuperation. Andy even learned how to give massages so that he could ease his friend's pain. For a time, Jim recovered and returned to his home. Though separated and with their own families, the two roommates continued to correspond and meet with one another as frequently as possible. Because of mutual business interests, on occasion the two had the opportunity to travel and lecture together.

Eventually Jim had a relapse. The arthritis became so crippling that he underwent experimental medical treatments and test procedures in an effort to find relief. They were a failure. Not only did the arthritis remain, but some of the organs in his body began to fail. As time passed, he became extremely frail. After a while, he became so ill that it was evident he was going to die. One month before his death, Andy wrote him a final letter:

> For me, and I think for you also, our relationship has more and more taken on a timeless quality. The world as a point of expression as a place to test and try the principles which we have tried together many times, to make a part of the inner structure of our beings has not always been easy for either of us in any age . . . words—my words at least—will not be adequate to express the joy I have known in sharing AND IN CONTINUING TO SHARE the dreams of helping each other as God used our gifts—tarnished as they have been at times . . . My mind and my heart have never been far from [your] bedside. Love, [Andy]
>
> Case 849-76 Report File

Jim passed away on June 6, 1953, at the age of forty-five. With his death, Andy lost one of his dearest and closest friends.

6

Working with the Present

———

*A*ccording to Edgar Cayce, the Akashic Records constantly provide individuals with a wealth of data, influences, patterns, talents, and unresolved issues that they must deal with for their growth and development. Based on an individual's soul history, it is true that one might anticipate what *could* happen in the present due to those urges; however, it is generally impossible to state exactly what *would* happen in any given situation because of the individual's free will. In the language of the readings, "NO EXPERIENCE, no urge, no environ, may be greater than the WILL OF an entity." (954-1)

Cayce believed that whenever an individual used the will in a positive direction, he or she could overcome all manner of difficulty and literally change his or her life experience. Although this process of meeting one's self is constantly overseen by the Akashic Records, the attainment of personal awareness is dependent upon the individual. However, as stated previously, personal lessons are destined to be repeated until they are learned.

An analogy of this premise is comically portrayed in the movie *Groundhog Day*, in which Bill Murray plays an individual whose main purpose in life seems to be one of simply satisfying himself. One morning, Bill finds himself stuck in time so that each day when he awakens it is once again "groundhog day"—the day the groundhog looks for its shadow. However, even though each day is the same, Bill quickly discovers that the substance and quality of each specific day's events is totally dependent upon his choices and his interactions with others. After a long while of making deliberate and unintentional mistakes, he comes to a crossroads in his life and decides to do everything he can to "get it right," and make the day a positive one not only for himself but for those around him. Once he gets it right, he is no longer stuck in time and he is able to move forward with his life.

According to the Cayce material, our search for soul growth and individuality continually leads to times in our lives that may be thought of as a crossroads. These are situations in which we face choices, conditions, experiences, lessons, even people that can enable us to accomplish whatever is next on the soul's learning agenda. Depending upon the choices we make, we are led to another crossroads and another set of possible experiences. These crossroads correspond to times in our lives as cycles of possible development. The experiences we draw toward us (and the lessons that those experiences encompass) are dependent upon the choices we've made leading up to that moment.

In reading 5244-1, Cayce stated that the Akashic

Records are the "impressions made by what the entity has done about the law of cause and effect and its spiritual interpretation in its relationship to opportunities and individuals in the experiences in the earth." In another reading, 364-6, Cayce described this information as "the records upon the wings or the wheel of time itself." It is the source of all that individuals had accomplished in their sojourns through the universe, as well as all of the influences that have a bearing on the present.

A thirty-three-year-old psychologist (2410-1) was interested in knowing what direction his occupation would take him in life. Cayce told him that the outcome was totally dependent upon his own choices, his desires, his hopes, and his ideals. If the young man chose a path of material gain and personal fame, the substance of his life experience would be very different than if he chose one in which his main purpose was to assist and counsel those who came to him for help. The reading encouraged him to chose the latter, giving his clients the gift of hope as well as a renewed sense of personal spiritual awakening. If he did that, the reading said he would find "contentment of mind, peace within self, and the material things necessary for carrying same forward to the GLORY of God—not for [2410]."

In reading 1567-2, a woman was told that her soul had left its permanent record upon time and space. Although those records had an ongoing influence upon her, because each individual was a complex composition of every thought and experience, the patterns and urges which became most influential were entirely dependent upon where she "cast her lot" in the present. The choices she made in the present would have the greatest influence upon her life experience.

The importance of choice and one's personal involvement in cocreating the substance of her or his life was echoed in the reading for a sixty-three-year-old woman who wanted to know what work God had planned for her remaining years (505-4). Cayce stated that the better question was rather, "what have I thus far in my earthly experiences fitted myself to do that I may in the present give the better expression of God's love in the earth . . . ?" The individual who could best answer that question, ultimately, was the woman herself.

In a reading given to a forty-one-year-old woman, Cayce reminded her that there were patterns from the past that had to be met. There were also experiences in her life which were destined to occur; however, the choices she made and the things she applied would determine the potential realities which would become part of her enfolding life. The soul is constantly involved in this process of writing the record:

> These interpretations we choose, then, with the desire and purpose that this may be a helpful experience for the entity; enabling the entity to better fulfill those purposes for which it entered this present sojourn.
>
> It is true for the entity, and for most individual souls manifesting in the earth, that nothing, no meeting comes by chance. These are a design or pattern. These patterns, however, are laid out by the individual entity. For, there are laws . . .
>
> It is true, then, that there are latent and manifested urges, manifested abilities, manifested virtues, manifested faults, in the experience of each entity. These faults, these virtues may be pointed out, yet the usage, the application of same is of free will—that which is the universal gift to the souls of the children of men; that each entity may know it-

self to be itself and yet one with the universal cause.

Thus the pattern, the book of life is written by the entity in its use of truth, knowledge, wisdom, in its dealings with its fellow man through the material sojourns. Also during the interims between such sojourns there are consciousnesses, or awarenesses. For, the soul is eternal, it lives on, has a consciousness in the awarenesses of that which has been builded.

2620-2

Individuals who wish to discover what is written about themselves on the Akashic Records may not have to look very far for answers. Cayce told one woman (752-1) that the soul became aware of relevant information impressed on the Akashic Records whenever that individual applied whatever knowledge she or he possessed. Elsewhere, individuals were told that they couldn't help but encounter the information because "these records are NOT as pictures on a screen, not as written words, but are as active forces in the life of an entity" (288-27).

Carol Ann Liaros of New York and Mary Roach of Virginia are two contemporary professional intuitives who have built reputations for themselves because of their psychic abilities. Both Carol Ann and Mary access the Akashic Records as the source of their information, and each has discussed ways in which the records manifest in the lives of individuals.

Echoing Edgar Cayce's statement that the Akashic Records are everywhere, Mary Roach believes that "the Akashic information for each soul resides as a blueprint and can be manifested in such things as fingerprints, blood type, astrology, iridology, the enneagram, numerology, dreams, self-hypnosis, personal reveries, etc. The blueprint of one's real self is even contained within DNA. Everything about every individual's record is manifested repeatedly in his or her life in many different ways." In other words, many aspects of an individual's life act as a "hologram" for the Akashic Records—each piece contains the entire whole.

Carol Ann Liaros says that her personal experience giving readings suggests that an individual's aura is a personal manifestation of his or her Akashic Record. Much like a network computer system, it is possible to access from the aura anything contained within the central record itself. Whatever is going on in the person's life is evident in the aura. She states, "An individual's aura changes as his or her physical health or vitality changes." When she sees gray spots around the heart area, for example, she knows that the individual has had a heart attack or has some other problem with the heart.

Similarly, Edgar Cayce once wrote about his personal experience seeing the human aura:

> Ever since I can remember I have seen colors in connection with people. I do not remember a time when the human beings I encountered did not register on my retina with blues and greens and reds gently pouring from their heads and shoulders. It was a long time before I realized that other people did not see these colors; it was a long time before I heard the word aura, and learned to apply it to this phenomenon which to me was commonplace. I do not ever think of people except in connection with their auras; I see them change in my friends and loved ones as time goes by—sickness, dejection, love, fulfillment—these are all reflected in the aura, and for me the aura is the weathervane of the soul.
> *Auras* (A.R.E. Press, 1945)

It's important to note that individuals do not necessarily

need to see auras or visit a psychic in order to discern what the Akashic Records would have them accomplish at any given point in their lives. As one reading states:

> Wherever you are! Whether in Hartford or Sing Sing, or Kalamazoo or Timbuktu, it's one and the same! The Lord is God of the universe, wherever thou art! For each soul finds self in that place which it occupies in the present only by the grace of God. Then use that today, that period. If it is used properly, then the next is pointed out.
>
> 3356-1

Regardless of what relationship, experience, or challenge we are currently in, it is that very same experience which the Akashic Records have brought into manifestation. What we do with that situation remains a matter of free will, but the potential for soul growth is ever present. The readings suggest that as an individual does what he or she knows to do in the present, then the records will bring into manifestation whatever comes next on the soul's learning agenda. Cayce frequently stated, "Line upon line, precept upon precept."

Edgar Cayce did not have to be in the room with an individual in order to give a reading. Most of the readings were given at a distance. Whenever a reading was scheduled for a physical condition, the individual was simply told to remain at home during the appointment time so that Cayce's subconsciousness could tune in to her or his location. Over the years, however, a number of individuals forgot their appointment times or were delayed in arriving at the agreed location. This did not seem to interfere with Cayce's ability to provide the information. In these instances, he might begin the reading with something like "we find those *impressions of the*

body [author's emphasis]—don't find the body here"
(reading 174-1 and others) and then proceed to give the
information requested. Individuals leave behind some
type of energy impression, perhaps a remnant of their
aura, that can be accessed by a sensitive.

In his book, *Psychic Warrior*, David Morehouse dis-
cusses his experiences with "remote viewing" and his
ability to perceive impressions left by the past, the
present, and the future. Remote viewing, also known as
"mind travel," theoretically enables an individual to observe people or events at a distance in space or time.
Similar to receiving information contained in the Akashic
Records, remote viewing allows the traveler to acquire
firsthand perceptions that have been recorded by others. Just as the Edgar Cayce readings had suggested, in
David's experience, "the past was locked and the future
was an untethered fire hose rocking and swaying, constantly changing."

In her book, *Intuition Technologies*, Carol Ann Liaros
recalls the remote-viewing experience of a blind woman
named Lola. Fearful of traveling by herself to a strange
location, Lola decided to "mind travel" to the hotel
where she would be staying. To begin, Lola became comfortable in her Buffalo, New York, living room. She relaxed and began to use her imagination to perceive the
hotel in Washington, D.C. According to Carol Ann:

> First, she visualized the hotel and its surround-
> ings from a bird's-eye perspective, and then she
> projected herself to the hotel's lobby. Using her
> imagination and the power of her mind, she went
> through the lobby and took the elevator to the floor
> where her room was located. She noted the floor
> number and projected herself down the hallway to
> her room. On entering, she paid special attention

to the layout, the placement of the furniture, even the colors of the room . . .

When Lola made her journey, she arrived at the very hotel she had seen in her imagination. She ended up on the same floor she had imagined as well, and discovered her room to be "exactly as she had visualized it several weeks earlier." (A present-day exercise in remote viewing is at the end of this chapter.)

Another method of obtaining personal information from the Akashic Records is through dreams. Just as dreams can be helpful in providing an individual with insights about her or his past experiences, the subconscious mind, in the dream state, has access to the records and is able to provide objective information about one's self in the present. For example, one woman had a dream in which a friend was speaking to her. She noticed that the woman had beautiful false teeth shaped like pearls and that every other tooth had the appearance of pure gold. Asked what the dream meant, she was told that the gold teeth represented the spiritual truths of which she was often speaking. The teeth were false, however, because she hadn't really applied in her own life what she was preaching to others (case 288-14).

An interesting dream occurred in the life of a young man named Henry, who was interested in spiritual growth. After attending an evening meeting in which participants discussed spiritual laws and personal transformation, Henry decided to "ask for a dream" about what he needed to work on spiritually. He related his experience as follows:

> I placed a notebook and a pen on my night table and wrote out the question: "What kind of guidance can I receive for personal spiritual growth?" A por-

tion of the dream I had that night was that I was in Egypt. William, an individual I admire for his insights, said that a man with the most beautiful eyes, surrounded by light, was waiting for me in a section of another one of the pyramids. I knew that the man was Jesus and that I was late because He had been waiting for me for a long, long time. I passed by my parents on the way, who, I think, told me to hurry. I got to the other pyramid and Jesus was indeed surrounded by light. He looked so loving and understanding and at the same time He looked so "at home" in the midst of all the people who sat around Him. He had me sit down next to Him and everyone began to ask me questions about dance steps that Jesus had apparently taught me and they asked me to please teach them what I had learned. I kind of remembered the fact that Jesus had taught me some dance steps, but I didn't remember what they were, yet I found myself telling everyone that I would go ahead and teach them what I had learned. Jesus looked at me lovingly from time to time, and once I had to stop myself when I realized that I was thinking an unkind thought about another person . . . Jesus looked up at me and reminded me of what I had been thinking, and told me that, more than anything else, *I needed to start working on my thoughts!*

Henry was convinced that the dream had provided him with a direct response to his question.

In 1932, while giving a reading to an individual, Cayce had a dream in which he saw energy fields surrounding various cities. In the dream, he realized that the energy put off by each city had an effect upon his ability to provide individuals with information in a reading. Just as individuals had energy vibrations, or auras, cities appear to possess something similar. The dream seemed to emphasize Cayce's oft-repeated statement that "thoughts are things." From his perspective, thoughts are literally deeds in the mental realm that have an influence upon the material world. Cayce recalled the dream as follows:

> There were certain portions of the country that produced their own radiation; for instance, it would be very much easier to give a reading for an individual who was in the radiation that had to do with health, or healing; not necessarily in a hospital, but in a healing radiation—than it would be for an individual who was in purely a commercial radiation. I might be able to give a much better reading (as the illustration was made) for a person in Rochester, N.Y., than one in Chicago, Ill., because the vibrations of Rochester were very much higher than the vibrations of Chicago . . .
>
> Case 294-131 Report File

The concept that individuals in similar circumstances can create an energetic effect upon mass consciousness as a whole appears related to the work of scientist Rupert Sheldrake. Sheldrake's theory of the existence of morphogenetic fields suggests that individuals are often influenced by unseen forces which can eventually impact their individual consciousness. In some respects, these "fields" sound remarkably like the Akashic Records.

During the course of one reading, in addition to discussing past-life influences and the importance of free will—"no urge, no influence is greater than the birthright of the entity—the will," Cayce made a statement which may have a striking connection to what makes the near-death experience even possible. The reading states in part:

The records are upon time and space, which are manifestations of that influence or force we call God. They are both old and ever new. But only in patience does the finite mind become aware of the VALUE of same upon the infinite, or the spiritual self.

Thus the records are taken from this skein of time and space. **Hence, as an entity enters and leaves consciousness in materiality, there is left upon time and space that which has been the activity— thus there may be the interpreting of same.** [Author's emphasis]

2144-1

The existence of the near-death experience was first brought to the attention of the public in 1975 by Dr. Raymond A. Moody, Jr.,'s international bestseller, *Life After Life*. In it, Dr. Moody explains that individuals who clinically "die" and are subsequently revived frequently share a common experience. Part of that experience includes seeing "a panoramic, instantaneous playback of the major events of his [or her] life." Is it possible that anyone having a near-death experience is actually reviewing the information contained within her or his own Akashic Record?

Perhaps Edgar Cayce was correct: "the records are everywhere." Each one of us is like a computer terminal plugged into the Akashic Records themselves. We can access the central database through our dreams, through imaginative reveries (one follows at the end of this chapter), through the aid and assistance of a reputable psychic, through some of the esoteric sciences (such as astrology and numerology), and other legitimate means. Other pathways include meditation and prayer, which Cayce believed were two of the greatest tools for cultivating personal serenity—a necessary skill for those who would experience "patience," described as the state of mind in which "all things will be brought to your remembrance."

However, perceiving the records themselves is not necessary in order for us to experience the urges and inclinations they contain. Regardless of where we presently find ourselves in life, we are in the midst of "meeting" those very impressions we have created upon the universe's database. Everything the soul experiences happens for a reason—whether or not we choose to become conscious of the lesson involved just yet is a matter of free will, but the lesson eventually will be ours to learn.

The Akashic Records are the impulse that draws to us exactly what we need, exactly when we need it. They are the force that brings individuals together to learn from one another. They are the tool which enables individuals to meet themselves and to become the very best that they can be. They are the universe's supercomputer system—perfectly keeping track of everything and releasing the data in perfect timing. And according to Edgar Cayce, they are not simply some philosophical concept, but are as real as anything which one might see with one's very own eyes:

> The entity should know that the record is as real as is that which may be indicated by that given off as light, for it goes on and on upon the etheronic energies and is recorded upon the film of time and space.
>
> 871-1

Everything about any individual who has ever lived is written upon the Book of Life itself.

Present-Day Imaginative Patterns Reverie

Note: A reverie is best done with another person (reading the reverie like a script) or with you first narrating the reverie on a tape and then playing it back in order to experience the exercise. This exercise is designed for individuals who wish to obtain insights into various common patterns of human experience. Reveries are generally narrated at about one-third the normal rate of speech.

NARRATION:

Relaxation Exercise:

Note: This relaxation exercise can also be used in preparation for the Remote-Viewing Experience which follows the Patterns reverie.

Become comfortable and relaxed and begin focusing your attention on your breathing. Let your awareness begin to notice how cool the air feels as you inhale and how warm it feels as you breathe out. After a few moments, bring your attention to your feet and ankles. Continue to breathe in, imagining the breath flowing through your feet, making them feel totally relaxed. Gradually bring this peaceful awareness up into your legs, remaining conscious of your breath. Notice how your breath is very soothing and relaxing, and that you are beginning to feel very much at peace.

Next, let your awareness move to your hips and your stomach. Your breath flows freely to that area—consciously breathe in deeply, and exhale slowly. Imagine that your breath is a beautiful golden (or white) light, constantly filling your body and bringing you into a deeper sense of peace. When your hips and stomach feel relaxed, move your attention next to your arms—the light spreading through them, making them feel lighter and free from any strain.

Your breath (and the sense of peace and relaxation) moves across your shoulders and up into your neck. Breathe in and feel its gentleness release any tension you might have in that area.

Slowly, it travels up your spine into your head . . . your facial muscles becoming totally at peace and relaxed. You feel very calm, quiet, and free from stress.

Take a deep breath, and focus on the sound of my voice. I'm going to help you get into a relaxed state of self-hypnosis. You're going to experience an imaginative reverie and you will be in complete control the whole time. In fact, you will be aware of everything that is going on around you. The first stage of self-hypnosis is actually a state of *attentive-relaxation* where your mind can become completely focused. It's a state where your imagination becomes more active, and your conscious mind becomes more relaxed. Now become completely comfortable . . . don't worry about moving about occasionally. Begin to breathe a little deeper and more easily. Just relax.

So you know what relaxation feels like, begin to tense up all of the muscles of your body. Focus on tensing (or "scrunching up") the muscles of your hands and arms and feet and legs and neck and head. Tense up everything real tight right now, and hold it. Then slowly let everything relax. Feel the relaxation flow through your entire body . . . through your head and neck. Feel the relaxation in your shoulders, arms, and hands. Feel the relaxation in your back, legs, and feet. Become more comfortable, and just let the relaxation flow through you . . .

Begin to breathe the way you imagine that you breathe when you are sleeping. And with every breath you exhale, you breathe out tension . . . worries . . . fears . . . anger . . . irritation. Breathe out all that troubles you, and breathe in relaxation. Breathe out anything that you'd like to get rid of right now. Breathe in relaxation, and become calm and in complete control. Take a moment to breathe slowly and deeply, letting your body relax.

Patterns reverie:

For just a moment, pause and relax. Take another deep breath, let your mind wander and your imagination flow and allow yourself to feel the first pattern of human experience.

When I count to three, you'll find yourself at a point somewhere in your current lifetime *when you experienced confusion or doubt about what you were doing.* Maybe it was a period when you weren't certain what to do with your life. It may be right now, or it may be a time in the past. When I count to three, your imagination will let you reexperience this time of confusion and doubt . . . One . . . two . . . three . . . Where are you . . . ? What's happening . . . ? What is it about this time that is so confusing . . . ? Do you feel alone, or do you feel like there's someone who can help you . . . ? For a few moments experience this time of confusion . . . don't analyze it . . . just experience it . . . [pause for 10 seconds]

Now, see if your imagination can tell you what this period was all about. What were you really supposed to be learning from this experience . . . ? Is it possible to take another look at this time in your life and discover a reason for it . . . or some value in it . . . ? Is there some way that confusion actually ended up helping you . . . ? [pause for 10 seconds]

Each of us has periods in our lives where we feel the need to build ourselves up physically, mentally, or spiritually. It might be a time when you placed greater focus on exercise or diet . . . Maybe it was a time of personal contemplation or learning . . . Perhaps it was a period in your life when you spent time in prayer or meditation . . . Whatever it was, when I count to three, you'll remember such an experience. One . . . two . . . three . . . Remember it now . . . [pause for 10 seconds] Can you feel how this time helped to invigorate your body, your mind, or your soul . . . ? Do you feel somehow "lighter" for having gone through the experience . . . ? [pause for 10 seconds] Ask yourself if the time has come, once again, for a similar period in your life . . .

Oftentimes, *people with different feelings and personalities struggle to come together in a common goal.* Maybe it's at work . . . or maybe it's at home . . . but you have a time like that in your own life . . . Imagine one now. One . . . two . . . three . . . What is happening . . . ? Do others sense that there's some kind of problem, or is it just you . . . ? For a few moments, look at a person with whom you've struggled and see the problem . . . don't analyze, just take it all in . . . [pause for 10 seconds] Now, in your imagination, find a common purpose (or an ideal) that you can agree on. Can you see how people can have their own thoughts about what needs to be done even though there may be only one activity or situation? Imagine what it would be like to find a unity of purpose with this other person . . . Take hold of this feeling of unity . . . [pause for 10 seconds] See if you can keep it with you . . .

Finally, when I count to three, I want you to imagine a situation in your life right now *where you have the opportunity to be of service to someone else.* Maybe it's only a kind word, perhaps it's a listening ear. Is there someone in your life whom you can help? Think of that individual now. One . . . two . . . three . . . Who is this person? What is it you can do to assist that person? [pause for 10 seconds] Okay, in your imagination, imagine helping that individual unconditionally. How does it feel to help someone who needs you . . . ? [pause for 10 seconds]

Okay, take a couple of moments now to reflect upon all that you've seen . . . and all that you've felt. Take it all in . . . [pause for 10 seconds]

Begin to tell yourself how well you will feel when you come out of this experience. When I count to three, you'll return to the present and begin to awaken at your own speed. Don't open your eyes until it's time, and when it's time, open your eyes gently and easily . . . Okay. One . . . Two . . . Three . . . Gently begin to wake yourself up at your own speed, until you're awake and totally refreshed . . . [pause]

Okay, open your eyes.

Please note: You may wish to record your experience somewhere while it is still fresh in your mind. Later, you can rewrite portions of this reverie in order to experience whatever patterns of human experience you think are important.

Optional Remote-Viewing Experience
This exercise is designed to give individuals a basic experience in "mind travel"—using their imagination to visit a location they have never been. The exercise focuses on a visit to the Edgar Cayce Foundation (the Association for

Research and Enlightenment, Inc., A.R.E.) in Virginia Beach, Virginia. Much like a reverie, you may wish to do this exercise with another person reading the script, or with you narrating it on a tape and then playing it back.

NARRATION:

Note: You may wish to begin with the relaxation exercise which precedes the Patterns reverie.

Close your eyes. Become comfortable and relaxed and begin breathing the way you imagine you breathe in your sleep. When you are ready, imagine that you are standing out in front of your house or apartment building looking up at the entrance . . . Visualize where you live . . . Can you see it? [pause for 10 seconds] Next, imagine yourself floating over your neighborhood or street. Look down at your surroundings and see what they look like . . .

When you are ready, imagine yourself floating over your city or town. What do things look like from this perspective . . . ? [pause for 10 seconds] Next, tell yourself that you want to imagine what it looks like to float above the East Coast—just above the shoreline of the Atlantic Ocean . . . What do you see . . . ? Is the water calm or rough . . . ? Are there seagulls? Can you see any dolphins playing? Can you see the surf? Are there people at the beach . . . ?

In your imagination, tell yourself that you are floating above the shoreline of Virginia Beach, Virginia. Across the street from the ocean you notice a large, brown, three-story, rectangular building. It's the Edgar Cayce Association, located at 67th Street and Atlantic Avenue . . . Can you see the main building . . . ? Can you see the meditation garden just behind the main building . . . ? Can you see other buildings on the property . . . ? [pause for 10 seconds]

Now, in your imagination, lower yourself to the front door of the main building. What do the doors look like? Can you feel the handle as you reach up, open the door, and walk inside . . . ? Look around the main lobby of the Visitor's Center. What do you see . . . ? Do you see the bookstore off to your right? Can you see other people? What color is the carpet? Are there any pictures on the walls? Look around the first floor of the building, taking note of who and what you see . . . [pause for 10 seconds]

When you are ready, in your imagination walk up the stairs in the lobby to the second floor . . . You'll pass through another doorway . . . Look to your left and to your right, what do you see . . . ? Can you see any displays . . . ? Can you find the library? Do you see all the books? Imagine yourself going into the library and selecting a special book . . . Pick the book up in your hands and look at it. Can you see what the title is about . . . ? [pause for 10 seconds] Is there a reason you selected this particular volume? Is there something about this book that you need at this time . . . ?

Now, in your imagination, leave the library and go out to the restrooms located on the second floor. Across from the restrooms, you'll find the third-floor stairway which will take you up to the meditation room . . . When you get to the meditation room, look all around . . . Can you feel the peacefulness of this place . . . ? [pause for 10 seconds] Can you see the colors . . . ? Do you see the stained-glass windows on one side of the room . . . ? Can you see the Atlantic Ocean through the third-floor window . . . ?

When you are ready, project yourself through the window and back over the Atlantic Ocean . . . Imagine that you're going home the same way you arrived . . . Imagine the shoreline of the East Coast . . . Imagine your own hometown or city . . . Imagine the house or apartment where you live . . . Imagine staring up at your entrance . . . Finally, imagine yourself sitting back down in your own room . . . [pause for 10 seconds]

Remind yourself that you have returned to the same place you started . . . And when you are ready, take a deep breath and open your eyes, feeling completely normal, refreshed, and relaxed . . .

Please note: You may wish to record your experience somewhere while it is still fresh in your mind.

Part Three:

The Future

~

The Spirit stood among the graves, and pointed down
to one. He advanced toward it, trembling. The
Phantom was exactly as it had been, but he dreaded
that he saw new meaning in its solemn shape.

"Before I draw nearer to that stone to which you point,"
said Scrooge, "answer me one question. Are these the
shadows of the things that Will be or are they
shadows of things that May be, only?"

Still the Ghost pointed downward to the grave by which
it stood.

"Men's courses will foreshadow certain ends, to which,
if persevered in, they must lead," said Scrooge. "But
if the courses be departed from, the ends will change.
Say it is thus with what you show me . . . Assure me
that I yet may change these shadows you have shown
me, by an altered life!"

Charles Dickens's *A Christmas Carol*

7

The Akashic Records and Probabilities and Potentials

—•◦•—

In giving that which may be helpful for the entity in its present development, much of every nature crowds in to be told; for the pages that are written, the influences that have borne upon the activities of the entity are many. These are as interpretations of that recorded here, which—if applied in the experience of the entity in the present—will bring those things into manifestations through activities that will be of helpfulness to the entity, as we see, in its soul development.

707-1

*I*magine that a software program had been created which could predict with astonishing accuracy the outcome of any decision or choice that you needed to make.

Not only could this program foresee your personal future, but somehow it could analyze the consequence of your choices and the effect those choices would have upon the people and events around you. Imagine, as well, that this program was so finely tuned that it could also correctly anticipate how the slightest change in your thoughts, activities, or decisions would impact any of the potential futures which had been envisioned. Finally, imagine that this ongoing process of calculating probabilities and evolving time lines takes place to draw together individuals and events to best provide everyone with the needed opportunities to learn the necessary lessons for personal transformation and soul growth.

From the perspective of the Edgar Cayce material, this complex calculation of evolving probabilities is essentially what occurs within the Akashic Records. However, it's not that the records are concerned with predicting the future; rather, their function is the analysis and tracking of individual and collective opportunities for soul growth. The future is not unmoving or predestined. It is dependent upon one choice leading to another and then another. From this standpoint, the outcome of one's "destiny" is only determined by how individuals utilize their free will in relationship to this vast supply of data and available information.

Whenever he gave readings, Cayce reminded the individuals that he was selecting the very information from the Akashic Records which would best enable them to fulfill the purpose for which they had entered the earth, "For each soul enters each experience for a development" (1235-1). Ultimately, it is the soul's desire that the development be achieved. However, each person possesses such a complex accumulation of conflicting emotions, behaviors, and patterns that the outcome is totally dependent upon the individual.

In 1941 Edgar Cayce told a fifty-two-year-old drama teacher (2630-1) that, when viewing her records, he became conscious of two very distinct possibilities for her life, "one that might have been, one that is." Because she had made certain choices, her life had moved in a direction where she could gain the most by helping others in her teaching position. Within her soul were also abilities which would enable her to bring spiritual truths and freedom of thought to other people. Suggesting that opportunities are never lost, Cayce stated that at some point in time the two opportunities for her life would merge into one; if not in this life, the integration would happen in the next.

The soul's passage through time and space is the method by which individuals grow in consciousness. What is most important about any single lifetime is what individuals do with the opportunities which present themselves from the evolving storehouse of the Akashic Records. Cayce told one individual that although the person had managed to apply spiritual truths throughout his soul's history beginning in 1472 in India, he had "lost" potential growth because of his inability to continue to apply spiritual principles whenever he experienced oppression of any kind. If he were unable to overcome this tendency in his present lifetime, as far as the records were concerned, he would have the chance to overcome it in the next (4349-1). A seventy-year-old retired farmer was told that his knowledge of government, people, and the law would—in all likelihood—manifest in his next lifetime when he would be given the opportunity to be a lawyer (304-5).

It's important to point out that the Edgar Cayce readings did not see one's identity as beginning at the moment of physical birth and ending some seventy to ninety years later. Individuals are not currently suffering from the karmic misdeeds of somebody else or somehow reaping the benefits of selfless acts performed by another. The soul's growth is an ongoing developmental process. The readings told one individual (4719-1) to just keep applying what he knew to do in this life so that in his next lifetime he would find himself even closer to the Creative Forces. The same talents, feelings, habits, and innate urges continue to be a part of the individual. The soul constantly meets itself. Whether an individual decides to overcome his or her remaining faults or to magnify his or her talents or virtues in order to assist others is what freedom of choice is all about. In any one life, an individual essentially "picks up" where she or he left off. In 1939, while viewing the records for one woman, Cayce told her:

> Remember, these interpretations are given with that intent to bring the materialization and realization to the entity of the continuity of life, and that what we do in mind and body records or leaves its imprint upon the soul—just as that one masticates in bodily functions produces the physiognomy of the individual.
>
> 1904-2

An amazing verification of this "continuity of life" would become evident in the case of a fifteen-day-old baby girl. In October 1939 Cayce told the parents that their baby had been Frances Willard (1839-1898) in her most recent lifetime. Frances Willard was a driving force in both the women's and temperance movements of the nineteenth century. By all accounts, she was a brilliant orator, a successful lobbyist, and extremely devoted to human rights, helping the poor and underprivileged. Although the parents of the little girl, Patty [2015], were open to the possibility that their daughter had once been the suffragette, both thought it best to withhold the information (and the reading) from the child until she was older. In fact, Patty wasn't told of the reading until she was sixteen years old.

At age thirty-one, Patty began to compile the striking similarities between her own life and the life of the nineteenth-century woman. The data became so convincing that author Jeffrey Furst worked with Patty to write a book detailing their investigation and its results. With the book's release, *The Return of Frances Willard* (1971), the publishers stated:

> Not only do Frances and [2015] share a strong physical resemblance and an uncanny likeness in personality, but a comparison of the lives of the two women, born *exactly* one hundred years [and a day] apart, uncovers startling parallels and, perhaps even more significant, a clearly defined pattern of continuity that makes the case for reincarnation still more profoundly convincing.

In addition to physical appearance, bone structure, and manner of speech, Patty resembled Frances in her feelings, beliefs, and desires. At the age of three or four, Patty had demanded to be taken to the polls with her father to vote. She frequently sang "Rock of Ages," Frances Willard's favorite hymn. She surprised her parents with her wish to be cremated, which Frances had desired and received. Throughout her childhood, Patty would often climb on top of any box she could find and "lecture" to an invisible audience—Frances spent a lifetime as an accomplished speaker. As a young woman, Patty was thrilled to cover her walls with Japanese watercolors, picturing the months of the year. The same pictures were hanging in Frances Willard's Oberlin, Ohio, home when Patty and her husband visited there. For years, Patty had wanted to find a black nineteenth-century English bicycle. Frances Willard had caused a stir a hundred years earlier by riding a similar bicycle when much of society believed that bicycling was "morally and medically wrong" for women. Both women were anemic, vegetarian, and religious. The list goes on and on. In the present, Patty had continued to focus her soul's interest in the direction of helping people. She was a volunteer social worker at a day-care center for underprivileged children.

The similarities between Frances Willard and Patty, her twentieth-century counterpart, are not to suggest that we are destined to eternally repeat the same patterns and inclinations. Instead, the soul is constantly in the process of evolving onward, but that evolution begins from the point where it left off. One reading states, "nothing is by chance, but is . . . a pattern of . . . the choices made by the entity in its relationships to things, conditions, and [other] entities" (1825-1). Progressive change is possible as individuals apply what they know to do.

Cayce told a forty-year-old fireman that God was personally conscious of each person and eternally desired all individuals to grow in the awareness of His presence, "For He, thy God, hath need of thee." The reading went on to suggest that each individual, regardless of phase of development, has the opportunity to be a channel of the Creator's consciousness, the Creator's activity, even the Creator's love in the individual's relationships with others. As to the manner of this growth in consciousness:

> For it is line upon line, precept upon precept, here a little, there a little, not some great deed to be done, some great thing to be performed, but ye

grow in grace, in knowledge, in understanding. Ye grow in making thyself a good husband, a good father, a good citizen. Not that ye become one suddenly because you've reached a certain age, position or place, because of thy financial or social position ... These ye attain by practice ...

But live the life for thy son, for thy neighbor, for thy brother, for thy friend, for thy foe. For this must be the consciousness in thee, that this is God's earth, God's world, God's consciousness that must be made manifest among men.

Begin in thine own self and with the one next to thee, and that which is not applicable in the life of thy son, of thy wife, of thy brother, ye cannot apply in a universal sense. Begin with self. Find the peace in self and ye will find that ye can bring it to others.

3902-2

Repeatedly the readings reminded individuals that they really knew what to do with their lives. They knew how to become better people through the application of spiritual principles and ideals. Unfortunately, too often there is a gap between knowledge and application. From Cayce's perspective, however, free will does not suggest that individuals get to choose *what* they wish to learn. That is part of the soul's involvement with the records themselves. Ultimately, freedom of choice simply allows individuals to decide *when* they will be successful with a particular lesson.

Because so many of her lessons had been met or overcome, the reading for a female biochemist (2396-2) states that there were few lifetimes currently impacting her present experience. In fact, her reading only provided her with three previous incarnations: she had been a Native American, gaining a love of nature and an awareness of plants and their medicinal properties; in Persia she had been known for her skills as (what might be called in the present) a dietitian, counseling individuals in the respective values of food and drink; and in Egypt she had focused on healing and rejuvenation. She was very intelligent. She was sympathetic and loving toward others. She was exacting in her ability to handle problems. Although the woman had overcome much and learned a great deal as a soul, Cayce stated that there were still additional lessons which would eventually unfold. The woman still had much to learn. The Akashic Records had simply set aside these additional lessons for what her reading called "future references."

Individuals sometimes have the mistaken assumption that when they are doing "what they're supposed to be doing," their lives will somehow be easy. From the wealth of case histories in the Edgar Cayce files, it becomes evident that this is not necessarily true. For example, just because an individual possesses an innate soul talent from the past does not imply that the ability will be easy to manifest in the present or the future. In 1943 Cayce gave a reading for an eleven-year-old girl in which he stated:

> Music should be the life giving flow, the interpreting of the emotions—physical, mental—of the body. A little later we should find these expressions taking other forms than the piano, but this is the basis—the interpreting, the ability to interpret most to the types or classes of music. So, begin with this.
> . . . Music! History of, the activity of, all of those various forms. If you learn music, you'll learn history. If you learn music you'll learn mathematics. If you learn music, you'll learn most all there is to learn . . .
>
> 3053-3

At the time, Cayce had not been told that the girl had been taking piano for four years. As the reading had suggested, the child was definitely drawn to music. In spite of her love for the subject, she was highly critical of herself and her ability and would frequently become "very upset about things not going well, especially in my practicing." Her mother later reported that it was so difficult to cope with the girl's temperament. If it hadn't been for the reading's advice, she simply would have allowed her daughter to "slack up" as far as music was concerned. Apparently the young girl had a "terrific inferiority complex" that lasted until she was a grown woman. Her problems with self-esteem were frequently magnified by those around her who believed she was odd or somehow different.

From the woman's own account, her life was frequently challenging. However, instead of allowing her feelings of inferiority to get the best of her and cause her to set aside her music because it was somehow inadequate, she became all the more intent on succeeding. In part, the determination enabled her to overcome her problems with self-esteem. Music continued to be an important part of her life. In addition to her piano talent, in time she would become adept at the harp, the clarinet, and "most of the other types of instruments as a part of my curriculum . . . " When she was a grown woman, she would become an assistant director of the opera and an enthusiastic music teacher of public school children.

Rather than being exacting about an individual's accomplishments with her or his innate qualities and talents, the readings generally stated what the talent was, for example: "in writing," "in teaching," "in dance," "in drama," "in guiding and directing children," and the like. Whatever individuals chose to do with their abilities was a matter of free will. One woman spent years trying to conquer her dependence on alcohol. Finally, she found help in the form of Alcoholics Anonymous. As if seeing the woman's former confusion, Cayce began the reading by stating, "what a rocky record!" Although she had a number of problems to work with, she was told that her greatest success would be in the field of "writing, reporting, following through with things that have to do with the upbuilding of human relationships . . . " In this manner, she would have personal success "and contribute to the greater welfare of the many" (5075-1). A few years later the woman's talents would enable her to write an important primer on alcoholism. In addition to writing the book, she would continue her efforts in the early work of A.A. and be instrumental in helping to transform many individuals.

The importance of helping others was frequently cited as the means to overcome one's problems and difficulties. From Cayce's perspective, there was always someone to whom an individual could be of service. In fact, being of service to that one individual was how a soul could perhaps best serve its Creator. After all, that was an essential purpose of one's life. In 1943 a sixty-two-year-old woman had reached the point that she felt her life was over (69-6). Looking for insights into her future, she wanted to know how much longer she would be alive. Rather than focus on the end of her life, the reading told her that she needed to become aware that as long as she was in the earth there was someone she could assist.

To clarify the laws governing reincarnation and a soul's evolving future, enthusiasts of the Cayce work asked in 1937 for a reading to help clarify "the laws governing the selection by an entity of time, place, race, color, sex, and the parents at any rebirth into the earth plane . . . " In response, the reading stated that the information was being taken from the records themselves. From that source, it became clear that each of these conditions was dependent on factors such as free will and what had been builded in a soul's experience (and therefore had to be met). However, the greatest determinant was those lessons which needed to be learned in a soul's particular phase of development. Whatever conditions had the greatest potential to bring to the soul's awareness what needed to be learned, those were the very conditions which were drawn together by the Akashic Records.

Later, in the same reading, Cayce was asked how individuals could become aware of their soul history and their records through space and time. His response was straightforward:

> By LIVING the record! For when the purposes of an entity or soul are the more and more in accord with that for which the entity has entered, then the soul-entity may take HOLD upon that which may bring to its remembrance that it was, where, when and how. Thinkest thou that the grain of corn has forgotten what manner of expression it has given? Think thou that ANY of the influences in nature that you see about you—the acorn, the oak, the elm, or the vine, or ANYTHING—has forgotten what manner of expression? Only man forgets!
>
> 294-189

Because of the challenges and pressures of everyday life, we might think that part of the "forgetting" is due to the sometimes overwhelming situations in which we find ourselves. And yet, from Cayce's perspective, it is only as we deal with those challenges in a constructive manner that the soul grows in its awareness. Perhaps one difficulty we face in our understanding is that we too often focus on "doing" rather than on the importance of "being." Essentially, the purpose of life demands a growth in consciousness and personal awareness. Yet, too often we become fixated on the goal or on our perception of what needs to be fixed or changed. We direct our energies into changing something (or someone) rather than on changing ourselves. We measure the success of our lives by our external accomplishments rather than by who we have become through the course of a lifetime of experiences.

The Akashic Records draw to us those circumstances, people, and events which have the potential to enable us to *become* more in attunement with the Creator. What we actually *do* with our lives may not be of great importance unless it assists others in their own process of becoming. This premise becomes clear in the Cayce readings on past lives. When discussing an individual's past personalities and identities, Cayce focused on what the soul had learned or become, *not* upon the individual's accomplishments in society.

Another difficulty we face in the modern era is our tendency to regard ourselves as being victimized by the people and the events which surround us. Too often, our challenges, our difficulties, and the ways in which our individual "lessons" manifest are seen as somehow being external to our own cocreative abilities. Unfortunately, this erroneous perception can have a detrimental effect upon our enfolding futures, and it is definitely not the perspective found in the Edgar Cayce material. *Everything* drawn to us had its origination in the Akashic Records, based upon our own previous adherence to or disregard of universal laws. Cayce told one woman:

In giving the interpretations of the records as we find them, upon the skein of time and space they are written ever by the mental and the material application of what the entity does about the spiritual influences in its experience . . .

If the constructive or creative forces are chosen, that are the manifestations of the Maker, the Creator, the Lord of the earth—yea, the universe, then man chooses the way that builds into the consciousness the awareness of that godly approach . . .

Those that choose for self that of fame, fortune or whatnot, that takes hold upon materiality alone, build that which becomes dross in the experience; and bring discomfort, disease, disturbance to the body and the mind, and—as it were shrivel or starve the soul.

1493-1

Even those individuals who received Cayce readings were not necessarily free from the tendency to believe themselves somehow victimized by life's experiences. In one instance, a twenty-five-year-old automobile salesman was given an overview of the negative and positive tendencies which were parts of his character. On the positive side, he was good with helping people, he loved spiritual ideas, he was talented with money, and he had innate abilities with machinery. Conversely, he was quick to anger, he was prone to "EXTREMES" in close personal relationships, and he had a predilection to be drawn into war. He was also very stubborn and his reading stated, "Woe are many, to many, that cross the entity's path when determination by the body is set in this or that direction."

In addition to advising how he might overcome some of his negative traits, Cayce counseled the young man that when he did marry he needed to remember that it was "a fifty-fifty proposition, and not a ninety percent proposition on the one side and ten on the other!" He was told to learn to adapt himself. In spite of the readings' advice, he apparently never saw his own responsibility in creating a successful relationship with another person. He married twelve years later and would eventually report back to Cayce's Association in 1957 how his life had enfolded:

> . . . I married twelve years following the date of this reading and stayed married one and one-half years. She was of the fair type. You won't believe this but one day I was walking down the hall and I saw this girl, and I said to the fellow walking with me, "I'm going to marry that girl." He said, "Do you know her?" and I said, "No." I found out where she worked, dated her some six months, and we were married. Not long thereafter she wanted to buy a home. I didn't. But we had to leave the apartment and get a home—wall to wall carpets, mirror over the mantle, etc., etc., so that I had to give up my boat and besides I lost $3,000 on the deal. You know, I grew to dislike this girl (she was from Georgia). Why wasn't the apartment all right? Anyhow, gradually I knew I was going to get out of this, and I did . . . I'm hard at work now in a Bank Clearing House . . . This Service where I'm working is an "information center" for banks. It's nice work, although working with twelve girls has its problems to say nothing of theirs.
>
> Case 1066-1 Report File

The past may predispose individuals to certain situations or events, but the ways in which they deal with the present is what determines the course of their futures. One startling example of this is the case of a seventeen-year-old boy who had a life reading in June 1937. Two years earlier a diving accident had left the young man a paraplegic, confined to a wheelchair. During the reading, Cayce told the boy's parents that the universe had entrusted to their care "a great soul that may give much to others [whenever] the earth and the things therein look dark" (1215-4). The soul had many talents: an aptitude for writing, great personal determination, and the ability to make the best of a bad situation. In terms of his cheerfulness and the acceptance of his physical condition, the reading even stated, "would that every soul would learn that lesson, even as well as this entity has gained in the present!" Cayce also reminded the parents, "Hence the purposes for each soul's experience in materiality are that the Book of Remembrance may be opened that the soul may know its relationship to its Maker."

What the Akashic Records revealed in this case were past lives which were having a "varying" effect upon the young man in the present. Previously he had been a soldier at Bunker Hill during the American Revolution. From this experience he had learned to be cheerful and to use whatever was at hand, making the best of a bad situation. From the same experience, he had acquired great personal fortitude and determination. Cayce pointed out that although his entire Revolutionary life-time had been one of material lack and deprivation as the world might measure success, he had made great strides both mentally and spiritually. However, it was the lifetime just prior to the Revolution which had drawn to him his present difficulty.

He had been a Roman soldier prone to self-indulgence, which accounted for his perpetual lack of material goods in the next experience. One of his favorite pastimes in Rome had been fighting in the arena. He loved the challenge of personal combat and felt great pleasure in beating his opponents. According to the readings, he went so far as to find glory in seeing the suffering of others:

> The entity saw suffering, and the entity made light of same.
> Hence the entity sees suffering in self in the present, and must again make light of same—but for a different purpose, for a different desire, for a different cause.

The young man was also given a past life in Arabia when he had gained abilities as a writer and a scribe. Cayce reminded the boy's parents that those same abilities could be drawn upon in the present.

When the parents asked about their son's life expectancy, the reply came, "This depends upon the application of that which is a part of the experience in the present. It should be many, many, many moons." When asked about his strengths and what they should expect of him, Cayce said:

> He may be a blessing to many. Do not count as man in multitudes but rather as God that looketh on the purposes and the desires of the individual soul, to make self as helpful, as hopeful to others, that they, too, may see the light—and the way.
> ALL! Expect all! As all life, all force, all power, all love is God—then there is a purpose, there is the expression of the will. Then keep it in that. For what ye expect, and ask for, that ye see, that ye experience.

When the reading was over, the boy's mother cried and said that it had been remarkable not only in its analysis of her son's strengths and weaknesses, but also in its attitude about the boy's future. A year later she would report:

> ... It is amazing and highly gratifying how understanding [my son] has become, and to him it seems the most natural development. But we can see the greatest contrast between the heedless, headstrong boy of yesterday and the patient, considerate boy he is now. And this experience has not in the least broken his spirit, for he is the strong character he always was, only his energy is directed in worthwhile channels. He is a great tease and quite a wit, so life is never dull, and he neither expects nor wants sympathy. In every sense of the word, "He can take it."

Eventually the boy would move out on his own to California, surround himself with friends and associates, and begin writing and editing a newsletter. By all accounts he got along extremely well, had a natural ability to write poetry and prose, and never saw himself as being victimized by his situation. In one of the final reports on file, his mother states: " ... he has grown to be one of the grandest people I have ever known, and will always be a force for good, no matter where he is placed."

From the thousands of individuals who had readings, it becomes apparent that the future is not simply a matter of fate, or chance, or luck, or even personal circumstance. It is a conditional event which is dependent upon individual and collective will. One's destiny is not determined by where an individual came from or where he or she might find him- or herself in the present. Instead, the future is dependent upon what one chooses to do with his or her current situation. At any moment in time, one's enfolding future might be cast as a shadow in a specific direction, but that shadow moves and bends as the individual changes her or his stance in the present. Day by day, choice by choice, each individual becomes personally responsible for the life she or he decides to lead. And every choice becomes a portion of the record, creating new shadows and impressions which may come to pass.

Even the finest computer system in the world would never be able to predict with complete accuracy the outcome of one's entire life when weighed against the possibilities and potentials of the human will.

8

Case Histories

*I*n spite of Edgar Cayce's accuracy in foreseeing future events, the readings are firm in their premise that the future is not "fixed." Each individual is ultimately responsible for creating and shaping the substance of her or his unfolding life. Frequently, Cayce would remind individuals of their cocreative responsibilities. Impressed upon the Akashic Records are an infinite number of future potentials for all individuals. These potentials, dependent upon one's urges, inclinations, past experiences, and talents, become real only as individuals utilize their free will in a specific direction. Ultimately, an individual's choices, relationships, and activities in the present set in motion a corresponding destiny. Rather than thinking there is only *one destiny for each individual*, it is more accurate to state that every decision in the present is destined to have a result upon that *one individual's unfolding future*.

While Edgar Cayce was alive, parents frequently obtained readings in order to best mold and shape their child's future. In addition to discussing past lives, abilities, and innate urges which were parts of the child's makeup, the reading frequently counseled parents in terms of education, direction, and upbringing. These suggestions were given in order to be "helpful and hopeful" and to best enable the child to fulfill those purposes for which he or she had entered the earth in the present. Frequently, Cayce reminded parents of their important cocreative role in helping to guide and direct their children. Nowhere was the importance of proper direction more stressed in the upbringing of a child than it was for Jimmy Hamilton [1208], born in 1936. One of the most fascinating aspects of this case is the wealth of documentation submitted over the years by Jimmy's parents, family members, and friends.

Two years before Jimmy was born, his parents Marie [934] and Ben [391] had met and fallen in love. The attraction between the two was overpowering. Marie was in the midst of ending an unhappy first marriage, and Ben appeared to be her knight in shining armor. A reading would later trace the attraction between the two to Greece. After Marie's divorce became final, the two married.

In spite of their immediate connection, the marriage was difficult from the very first. Both were strong-willed and unyielding. Two months after being married, the couple separated and Marie returned to her family in Ohio. Finding herself pregnant, Marie arranged to have an abortion. The pull each had on the other was unmistakable, however, and the couple reconciled within a few months. At the time, a reading on the relationship was obtained and Cayce told them that they could, in fact, work together. There was an obligation that each owed the other from the past. Ben and Marie needed to learn to be less willful and to compromise. The reading recommended that "Each should be a complement one TO the other. And this CAN be made true, if it will be worked together. It cannot be made true separated or apart!" (391-8)

The two managed to stay together until June of 1936 when their son, Jimmy, was born. Greatly interested in the work of Edgar Cayce, they obtained a reading for the boy when he was only two days old! The reading was fascinating and held great promise for the child.

Jimmy Hamilton's parents were told that their son had once been a skilled politician. The boy was so talented, in fact, that if he were directed in the proper channels, he could become one of the most influential political figures in the history of the United States. His education and training were of the utmost importance. Cayce went on to make a startling prediction for the baby. *If Jimmy were raised properly, the child's life would mean as much to a new world order as the life of Thomas Jefferson had meant to the founding of America.* The ultimate promise of the child's upbringing was that he would help to bring peace to the entire world, even to the point of unifying it as "one nation"!

However, foreseeing coming events, the reading warned the parents that the child's development could have some "peculiar or unusual turns." (1208-1) Unless guided aright, the opportunities for fame or defame "will be AS ONE." From experiences in Greece and Persia, the soul had acquired inclinations for self-indulgence. If these tendencies were not overcome in the present, it was possible that they would run wild in the child's future.

At least seven times in one reading, Cayce reminded the parents of their important role in guiding and directing this child. The boy was inventive and extremely inquisitive about people and the world around him. Turned into a negative direction, that inclination would create an individual who questioned and challenged everyone—a born "arguer," who loved to create opposition. He had high mental abilities—however his ingenuity could be as detrimental as it could be beneficial if not channeled in the right directions. Jimmy's reading stated that he belonged to the world and would "regard all peoples alike." He would have relationships with people all over the globe. There was no question that the reading foresaw great possibilities for the child.

Due to their personal difficulties, just two months later, in August 1936, the boy's mother separated from her husband. For a short time, Marie would take the child to Ohio. The couple reconciled shortly thereafter, but their problems were not solved. Eleven months after Jimmy's birth, the couple's unhappiness had become evident to both family and friends. In May 1937, the boy's aunt wrote, "His parents have managed to stay together, though there is a flare-up every now and then. I'm just praying and sitting tight." Mutual stubbornness between the two, as well as excessive drinking, only worsened their friction.

In 1940 Jimmy started kindergarten and loved it, but shortly thereafter his parents separated again and his mother took him back to Ohio. By May, the couple reconciled a third time and the family moved to Alabama. The same year, a close family friend visited from Virginia. After seeing young Jimmy and returning home, the friend wrote to Ben:

I hope, [Ben], you won't think me meddling when I say the things I am prompted to say here, from having been at your home . . . I was very much tempted to bring [Jimmy] home with me, but didn't think it was right to do so . . . as you know, we each of us here think as much of him as if he belonged to us, and it is because I'm anxious about his health that I'm saying this.

Case 391-1 Report File

By Christmas, Marie and Ben had separated again. Jimmy's mother took him back to Ohio. A couple of months later, she wrote:

I'm in an awful state of mind. I feel what I have done is right and yet I feel that [Ben] and I have failed each other. There's no doubt in my mind that we could have done better in regard to our advantages. It's too late now, so we must bear the best of it. There are times when I love him and miss him, and then again I feel resentful.

That same month, Ben submitted his own letter:

My life has really been a jumbled-up affair and naturally there are a lot of things I feel sorry about, especially my boy, but I'd rather not even think about it because it's a long, long way from the conditions I would like to exist.

Two months later, Ben told a friend, "I'm afraid I made a big mistake in not taking [Jimmy] away from her."

Marie and Ben were divorced in 1942. For a time, Ben moved overseas and Marie continued to struggle with the child's upbringing. That same year, when Jimmy was six, he would have another reading. The family friend who previously had shown concern about the boy had looked into the possibility of sending the boy away to school. The school, located in the Northeast, had an excellent reputation, and Marie asked about the advisability of sending her son. The reading encouraged Jimmy's mother to give her child the opportunity he so badly needed to express himself. The boy's abilities were still apparent. Cayce added that the school which had been selected was as near as ideal "as might well be imagined" and he emphasized, "THINK WHAT THE ENTITY MAY MEAN, CAN MEAN, TO SO MANY OTHERS!" (1208-18) Unfortunately, Marie changed her mind shortly thereafter. She did not want to send Jimmy away to school. The family friend noted:

> [Jimmy]'s mother got cold feet, said she couldn't bear to think of his being so far away from her when he was so young. Hard to say what is what—just hope she never regrets it. Am disappointed, yet not surprised, but she had been so willing when I made arrangements. Do not know what happened to her.
> Case 1208-1 Report File

In October of that year, his mother sent Jimmy to live with his Aunt Clara (Ben's sister) in Virginia. The arrangement seemed much better for him. He loved Clara deeply (and she him), and he enjoyed staying with her. He did well in school, making good grades. One of his favorite pastimes was to draw. However, four months later, Jimmy's mother wanted him back and he returned to live with her and go to a local school. He was not as happy. His report card indicated that he often annoyed others and made unnecessary noise in class.

Eight months later, Marie had a change of heart and

Jimmy was sent back to live with his aunt. However, by 1944 his mother had taken him yet again. For the next two years he would stay with Marie most of the time, but he was switched between public and private schools so often that he rarely stayed in one place for more than a few months.

In spite of their previous history, shortly after World War II ended, Jimmy's parents remarried. The marriage lasted a month. Both had alcohol problems which had grown during the years, and they quickly separated. In 1947 Jimmy changed school three times and was doing so poorly that the school recommended he repeat the fifth grade. Jimmy returned to live with his aunt. His school year between September 1947 and May 1948 was the only year he was able to "stay put" and finish in the same school he had started.

In May of 1948 his mother married another man and Jimmy went back to Ohio to live with her. The marriage (his mother's fourth to three different men) did not last long. The child was shuffled from one location to another throughout the time he was twelve and thirteen. Eventually, he returned to live with Clara.

In 1951, when Jimmy was fifteen, his aunt wrote: "This is a very critical time in his life, as you know. I'm not a good substitute for two parents, but I'm doing the best I can." She also noted that although he was not a good student, he excelled in sports and was very interested in music and art.

In 1953, when he was seventeen years old, instead of going to summer school to make up work he had failed, Jimmy Hamilton ran away with a friend to Florida. While there, he and the friend got into trouble for stealing, but were not punished because of the intervention of family friends and the fact that both boys were under age.

In 1955 Jimmy enlisted in the marine corps. The recruiting officer stated that the young man had received the highest mark of anyone in the city where he was recruited. Jimmy liked the marine corps very much and began to travel. Confirming Edgar Cayce's statement that he would "belong... to the world." (1208-1) From Japan, he wrote his aunt: "I wish it were possible for you . . . to visit Japan—it's such an amazing country...I don't know why I feel so much at home with these people." Foreign languages seemed to come easy to him.

When nearly twenty, his father—who had seen him only rarely over the years—wrote him a letter:

> I know that both of us would have wanted you to have a much nicer life than you did have but our own little petty likes and dislikes at the time were all important. Now they don't seem to be, but it's too late as far as you are concerned. The time when we both should have been with you, we were somewhere else. You know all this, but I want you to know that I know and realize it, too . . .

In 1960 Jimmy's parents discussed the possibility of yet another reconciliation, but it never happened. Ben married someone else and later separated.

After his stint in the marine corps, Jimmy moved to Los Angeles and began playing bass in a band. In time he would play in a jazz combo and, according to his aunt, he "enjoyed the Bohemian type of life." By 1959 he was in Florida selling commercials for radio and TV programs. By the end of the year he was back in Virginia and spent every spare moment of his time practicing in a jazz group. He married in 1960, at which point his wife put a stop to his musical ambitions and insisted that he settle down. They had a baby son two years later. During that time, he took some law courses but was never able to finish. In 1963, he had become an assistant manager of a clothing store. The following year, he picked up his life-long interest in art—hoping to go to night school, but his plans never materialized. In 1965, Jimmy and his first wife separated.

In 1966, Jimmy Hamilton married again and worked in a clothing store. That same year, his mother, Marie, stated that if she had been as wise twenty years earlier, she could have saved her marriage to Ben. In 1967 Jimmy and his wife had another child, but a year later they were divorced. He next moved to the Washington, D.C., area and managed a boutique. According to his Aunt Clara, for a time he sought out counseling in an effort to try to "get hold of myself." Eventually, he would marry and separate a third time.

By the fall of 1970 Jimmy had moved to Greece. He wrote his aunt, "I love it. We should all be Greeks again. It would do us good . . . Everyone loves everyone—no communications gap, no put-ons . . . I can't begin to explain the beauty of this new world where I am now living." By November he had moved to Italy and by December he traveled to Spain and Africa. Shortly thereafter, he returned to Virginia. In time, he would find a variety of jobs in both the clothing and restaurant businesses. He was personable and people liked him. And yet, although he was good with people from all different backgrounds, much of his life seemed spent in trying to find himself. At one point, a friend of his told his aunt that Jimmy's fantastic potential was evident to everyone around him, but that Jimmy's own fears and argumentative nature were leading to his undoing. In the end, he never did fulfill the political possibilities promised by the reading.

It is important to point out that although Jimmy Hamilton never fulfilled the extraordinary future once foreseen by Edgar Cayce, the path of his unfolding life was his own. The choices made by him and his family enabled him to have experiences and opportunities which still had the potential to be beneficial at a soul level. Each choice and decision simply created another set of probable realities that were drawn to him. Because of Jimmy's upbringing, a different possibility emerged from the Akashic Records, but it was a possibility based upon his own soul history, previous experiences, and ongoing decisions. The way individuals respond to each of those events and circumstances which they draw to themselves ultimately will determine the potential substance of their unfolding tomorrows.

Another interesting case is that of Patrick Thompson [641], who received a Cayce reading when he was fourteen years old. Although he was still a teenager, the death of his father had forced the young man to work to support his widowed mother and youngest sister. In spite of the family's financial problems and Patrick's heavy responsibilities at such a young age, his mother reported, "He never complains." He worked as a newspaper boy in a small Alabama town. Prompted by an older sister, Patrick obtained his reading in 1927.

Though he was mature beyond his years, Patrick's only weakness was a problem with digestion. Whenever he ate rich or sweet foods, he would become extremely ill and nauseated. As he grew up, he learned that he had to be very cautious in his personal diet. Not seeing it as a hardship, Patrick simply accepted the condition as being normal for him.

Cayce began the young man's reading by stating that most of Patrick's talents and latent urges had yet to manifest; however, they were definitely present and would begin to emerge "through the application of will." Among his qualities, Patrick was told that he was slow to anger, quick to make friends, and would find his greatest success in business relationships having to do with salesmanship. The reading advised that he would "find the greater success, the greater development in the present experience, coming through that of association with peoples—in the condition of the BUSINESS man, *especially that as pertains to materials, clothing, or of such natures.*" [Author's italics] His innate talents were especially suited in the area of personal attire. He was also told that he had a great love for spirituality and would find much personal fulfillment in those things which enabled him to find a greater sense of "attunement with the Divine."

His talents with clothing were traced to a lifetime in France when he had been among the personal staff and escorts of Louis XIII. At that time, Patrick had served as an adviser for the king's wardrobe. From the same period, he had acquired the ability to enter a room and leave and then could describe the dress of everyone present simply by recalling what he had seen. Cayce assured him that this ability remained with him because he possessed an innate love of materials and attire.

This same capacity with apparel had been evident in ancient Egypt when he had designed clothing for various groups and peoples as a method of designating one from another. In Atlantis, he had also been especially concerned with knowing various materials and their suitability for wearing apparel.

Patrick's problem with digestion had not been mentioned to Edgar Cayce previously, but it was pointed out during the reading. The young man was warned against overindulging in any food or drink. Apparently his sensitivity was the result of past actions. In France, when he had been adviser for the king's wardrobe, he had developed a serious problem with overindulgence and gluttony. In addition, in a lifetime as a court physician in

Persia, he also had been drawn to overeating and personal excess. His present problem, originating from the Akashic Records, was an effort to enable his personal weakness to be overcome in the present.

Although Patrick found the reading interesting, he had no desire to find work in the clothing industry. He therefore continued his job at the newspaper. In addition to his work and ongoing responsibilities as head of his family household, Patrick finished high school education and graduated at seventeen. He had always dreamed of going to college, but because he had to support his mother and sister, it just wasn't possible.

At the age of twenty-one, Patrick was promoted to the position of assistant circulation manager at the newspaper. Making only a modest salary, he had put aside any thoughts of marriage and having his own family because he couldn't support two households. To make matters worse, he was attempting to help his older sister's family financially since her husband was out of work. At the same time, a follow-up report was submitted to Cayce's Association.

Patrick reported that although he was interested in some kind of occupational change, he had no interest in seeking employment in the clothing business nor had he ever had any opportunities in that direction. He wondered why the reading had recommended a life's work that just didn't appeal to him. For several years, he had been seeking a more lucrative job—even practicing his typing and bookkeeping—but thus far, he had been unsuccessful. In an effort to get guidance in his present situation, Patrick asked for another reading.

When he asked, " . . . what line of work could I use my abilities to the best advantage?" (641-3) Cayce reminded him, "As indicated, in that line associated with cloths or things that have to do with wearing apparel." Confused as to why the reading continued to insist on something in which he had no connections, Patrick asked where he could seek out such employment. The answer was that he would find the connections he needed through "present associations."

Because of his faith in Mr. Cayce's abilities, shortly after the reading Patrick decided to begin writing letters to anyone he could think of in the clothing business. He sent applications to individuals and firms, giving them his background and work experience and stating that his desire was to change jobs and become a "salesman on the road for wearing apparel." For three years his efforts were not very successful. He supplemented his income with restaurant jobs and his position at the newspaper. Finally, in the spring of 1939, when he was twenty-four years old, he got the break he needed.

While he was visiting a large city, his older sister had encouraged him to call on some friends she knew. The friends were familiar with Edgar Cayce and had obtained readings of their own. In addition, for three generations the family had been in the clothing business, manufacturing uniforms. During the course of his visit, Patrick explained that he had also received readings from Cayce and that they had repeatedly emphasized his talent with clothing. His hosts needed no additional referral. Immediately, the family offered him a job as a traveling salesman and gave him his own territory of several Southern states. He became the youngest member of the firm's staff.

Patrick was immediately successful with his new position. He liked people and he seemed to have a special knack with cloth and materials. However, he was quickly turned off by the cut-throat business practices and the underhanded dealings which seemed to be a part of the business. Both were foreign to his own method of dealing with people. As if to confirm his direction, Patrick obtained another reading shortly thereafter and was reassured that according to the Akashic Records "This is still indicated as the greater activity for the entity, and in such associations the entity may find the greater outlet for the abilities . . . through relationships with garment making, clothing, dress . . . " (641-6) Patrick was encouraged to focus on his own spiritual ideal and to always remember that it wasn't so important how others treated him, but how he treated others, "Not so much that as ye would desire that others be, or that others might do for thee, but rather as to whether or not thy material or daily activity—in dealing with thy fellow men—is in keeping with thy spiritual ideal."

That same year he would tell his older sister that the spiritual advice in his reading had changed his whole outlook on the business world. He said that it enabled him to approach every person with a new frame of mind, whether the individual was a tough customer or an underhanded competitor. He became content with what he was doing, and his finances improved tremendously. Within one year, Patrick's success was so remarkable that his employers noted that he had a knack for handling customers which most of their experienced sales staff would never possess.

World War II ensued. Because of Patrick's food allergies and problems with digestion, he was classified 4-F and made the manager of clothing and uniforms at an army induction center, where more than fifteen hundred officers were outfitted each week. In 1944, when he was finally certain he could support his own family as well as his mother, he got married. He was thirty-one years old, at the time considered late to marry. When the war was over, he returned to his former position in the clothing business. Patrick and his wife would have three children.

He loved his job and his family. He and his wife maintained a lifelong interest in their church and, for the rest of his life, he would also remain a strong supporter of Edgar Cayce's Association, the A.R.E.

In 1965, at the age of fifty-two, Patrick visited the A.R.E. with his family. During the visit he explained that he was very successful as a sales representative in New York with the same company he had been with for more than twenty-five years. At the time, he stated that without the advice of the readings he would never have pursued a line of work which had given him such satisfaction. He was now in charge of the retail side of the business.

In 1971 he submitted an additional report. He had retired at fifty-eight, after being involved in the uniform business for more than thirty years. Toward the end of his career, his skills with people had made him responsible for the training of salesmen in the national organization. Just as Cayce had told him when he had been only fourteen, Patrick's occupational talents were in the direction of clothing and people. After his retirement, he would become involved, part-time, in real estate.

Later, while submitting one final report on the accuracy of the information which had been given to him by Edgar Cayce decades earlier, Patrick stated that the readings had led him "to a better understanding of the purpose of my life as being an opportunity for development and fulfillment . . . they brought me to the realization that in being of service to others in business relations was a positive opportunity to be helpful to all." From all accounts, Patrick was extremely successful at being true to his spiritual ideal and in sharing with others the very best that he had found within himself.

A final case is the story of Lucille Williams [499], whose parents were interested in Edgar Cayce's abilities and obtained a reading for their daughter and other family members. She was twenty-two years old at the time. Raised in a wealthy family, Lucille called herself a "New York socialite" and appeared to have all the advantages that money could buy. She was not really interested in the reading and years later, while being interviewed for an article ("Artist Fulfills Cayce Prediction"), she told a newspaper reporter "at the time he did it, it meant nothing to me. It went in one ear and out the other."

Lucille's reading stated that she was affable and that she made friends easily, she was very interested in people and was sentimental in matters of love. In the past she had been in Colonial America, Rome, Greece, and Egypt. She had been involved in helping people of various races get along. She had been a teacher whose primary skill enabled individuals to make permanent changes in their lives. Her soul also had innate abilities with healing.

Cayce remarked that she had a deep interest in spirituality and was a lover of nature and music. The reading suggested that her life would take a change and she would become very involved in "art and its relationships to activities in individuals' lives." Cayce stated that she would become fascinated with the medium of stained glass and the effect of light upon prisms of glass. Not showing interest in the information she had been given, after the reading Lucille left it with her parents where it was set aside. Six months later she married and settled with her husband to begin their family. Her contentment would be short-lived.

Although happy in her marriage, by the time Lucille's children were three and four, she felt driven to find some means of being fulfilled beyond her roles as wife and mother. She would later report to the A.R.E., "I was looking for something to keep my soul alive." Finally, she felt

SEEKING INFORMATION ON

holistic health, spirituality, dreams, intuition or ancient civilizations?

Call 1-800-723-1112, visit our Web site, or mail in this postage-paid card for a FREE catalog of books and membership information.

Name: _____

Address: _____

City: _____

State/Province: _____

Postal/Zip Code: _____ Country: _____

Association for Research and Enlightenment, Inc.
215 67th Street
Virginia Beach, VA 23451-2061

For faster service, call 1-800-723-1112.
www.edgarcayce.org

PBIN

"led by the nose" to a YWCA course in leaded glass. At the time there were few books available on learning the art of stained glass, but Lucille had the opportunity to come in contact with a number of masters in the field and began to teach herself. She came to cherish the craft as a demanding work of love.

Years later, when her mother died, Lucille was surprised to come across the reading which Edgar Cayce had given her. By 1946, in addition to her family, the three greatest loves of her life had become stained glass, music, and nature—each had been discussed in the reading. Because of her talent, Lucille would eventually gain quite a reputation in the field of stained glass windows. She reported on the events of her life in March 1977 and stated, "It might also be of interest to you that I am self taught in the field of stained glass, and have developed this original approach on my own that is quite different from anyone else's work, either in the U.S. or Europe. A number of books and magazines have given space to my techniques . . . "

Lucille went on to explain that she had been a student of voice and ballet and that she could play the piano and the organ—in fact, she insisted that she "could not live without music." She also tended a large garden and raised her own organic fruits and vegetables. Her stained-glass work had won awards at the Corcoran Gallery of Art and the National Collection of Fine Arts at the Smithsonian Institution. Because the reading so accurately depicted the individual she would become, in August 1977 Lucille and her husband visited the A.R.E. in order to take measurements for the two sets of stained-glass windows she wished to donate to the organization. When completed, each window consisted of three panels, measured twenty feet in length, and weighed three hundred pounds.

Lucille died in 1992 at the age of eighty. Her obituary is the final report in her case file:

[Lucille Williams], 80, a nationally known and widely exhibited stained-glass artist, died of natural causes March 4 at Greenwich Hospital. A resident of Greenwich for 33 years, she was creating stained-glass windows up to the time of her death. Her most recent installations were two windows at The Church of the Holy Comforter in Kenilworth, Ill. Regarded as a pioneer and innovator in the field of abstract stained-glass windows, [Mrs. Williams] received inquiries and requests for her windows from as far away as Saudi Arabia and India. While stained-glass windows are usually associated with cathedral windows depicting biblical scenes, hers are abstract designs using layers of different types of glass of varied shapes and colors. [She] had taught classes at the Greenwich YWCA and her work was shown in exhibits of The Greenwich Art Society and the Stamford Art Association. She was a member of the Stained-Glass Association of America, from which she received several first-place commendations. Locations of her glass installations include the Greenwich YWCA, the Cole Auditorium of the Greenwich Library, St. John's Episcopal Church in Stamford, The National Cathedral in Washington, D.C., The Connecticut Hospice in Branford, Concordia College in Bronxville, N.Y., and the Association for Research and Enlightenment Meditation Center in Virginia Beach, Va. Additionally, her works are part of the permanent collection of glass at the Corning Museum in Corning, N.Y. . . .

Case 499-2 Report File

9

Discovering Insights
into Your Future

---

*C*he variable nature of one's future is graphically
portrayed in the motion picture *Back to the Future II* with
Michael J. Fox. Fox plays a young man, Marty, who is suddenly thrust into a horrific future which bears little re-
semblance to the life he knew. In a short time, Marty
comes to the realization that "the future" in which he
finds himself has been built upon a series of events that
took place in his own past. In order to change the future,
he needs to return to the past and rectify his misdeeds.
Thankfully, the young man has at his disposal a time
machine and he is able to go back and correct what went
wrong. Once that is accomplished, the future he found
so appalling suddenly ceases to exist.

Even without a time machine, *the future is ever*

changeable. Because of the vital role free will plays in our lives, no other statement is more useful in summarizing the readings' outlook on our enfolding tomorrows. Beyond the soul's tendencies, talents, and innate urges, nothing is predestined or set. Although these urges may sometimes predispose an individual in a certain direction, the outcome of her or his life is integrally connected to the will. The Akashic Records provide all individuals with those very circumstances and events which will best enable the soul to have the greatest probability for success.

Edgar Cayce repeatedly reminded people they could be successful—in terms of soul growth and personal transformation—if they simply applied whatever it was that they knew to do. Most often, individuals are aware of some of those very things which would enable them to become better people. However, too often there is a gap between knowledge and its application. The readings frequently admonished individuals to "do what you know to do and the next step will be given." In other words, soul growth is not dependent upon what an individual knows; instead, it is predicated upon what an individual does about what she or he knows. In the language of the readings, " . . . O that all would realize, come to the consciousness that what we are—in any given experience, or time—is the combined results of what we have done about the ideals that we have set!" (1549-1)

Simply stated, an ideal is the motivating influence that undergirds the intentionality of *why* an individual does what he or she does. The focus is upon one's intent. Rather than it being an intellectual exercise, Cayce encouraged individuals to choose ideals which would enable them to apply the qualities of love, service, compassion, and understanding in their interactions with others—all the while becoming better people in the process. Essentially, a spiritual ideal causes individuals to be concerned with how they might assist those around them. The focus is on others rather than upon one's self.

The importance of becoming aware of one's intent and choosing a spiritual ideal is to enable individuals to become aware of what they are building and inscribing upon the Akashic Records. As far as the readings are concerned, the future of each individual is destined to include meeting those very conditions which she or he has built in the past and is continually building in the present.

Because of the changeable nature of one's destiny, individuals might wish to know how it's possible to gain insights into their evolving futures. From the readings' perspective, there are at least two facts of which an individual can become certain. The first is that the soul is destined to grow (and eventually awaken) to an awareness of its true relationship to the Creator. Whatever it takes to bring about this growth in consciousness is exactly what the Akashic Records will continually draw toward the soul. Cayce asked one individual, how much longer "Can the will of man continue to defy its Maker?" (826-8) In terms of one's personal future, the second certainty is that individuals will continue to draw a particular lesson toward themselves until they have learned it. This second premise is clearly illustrated in the work history of Glen Peters, a businessman:

Glen started a new job at a company and found himself sharing office space with a woman named Tammy. From the first, Glen didn't really care for his office mate. He felt that she talked too much, seemed very jealous of his arrival, and appeared intent on guiding and overseeing his work, thereby (from his perspective) preventing mistakes he might make due to his inexperience with the company. Over several months, the situation worsened until Glen could no longer stand being in the same room with her. It caused him greater frustration to realize that no one else in the office had as difficult a time with Tammy as he did. A number of people genuinely liked her, so complaining to his boss seemed somewhat childish. During one weekend, when he was pondering what to do in his situation, an insight finally came to him.

In thinking about his work history, Glen realized that in his last two positions, "at two different companies," he was in situations in which he had been forced to interact on a regular basis with two different personalities "exactly like Tammy." It was this recognition which made him realize—somewhat reluctantly—that he was the one who needed to change, not his office mate. From then on, Glen did whatever he could to interact with Tammy on a positive basis.

He decided that her talkative nature and unwelcomed "critiques" were possibly in response to the fact that he rarely shared his thoughts on any company project. The same had been true at his previous places of employment. He surmised that Tammy's perception of his inexperience was either caused by his projecting a "know-it-all" attitude (even when he didn't) or a result of her feelings of inadequacy. Either way, Glen felt that part of the solution was to engage with her more frequently and to find occasion to honestly admire her work.

By his admission, healing the relationship was not always easy, for he frequently found himself falling into old patterns of behavior. But in time there was a definite change and his entire perception of Tammy changed as well. He was genuinely surprised to find that he liked working with her and even considered her "a friend." In relating the story of his work history, it became apparent that the Akashic Records had drawn the same situation to Glen twice previously before he was finally able to effect a change in his own awareness. From the perspective of the Edgar Cayce readings, lessons that have been ignored or avoided are destined to become a part of one's personal future.

The same tools that can assist individuals in gaining insights into the Akashic Records dealing with their past and present are helpful in enabling them to perceive glimpses into their evolving futures. The esoteric sciences can be valuable as long as individuals keep in mind that their future is not fixed regardless of what anyone might believe to the contrary. To be sure, there are "potential patterns" in one's life, but what an individual does with those patterns and where she or he directs her or his life energies is a matter of free will.

Personal reveries (one is included at the end of this chapter) and dreams can assist individuals in gaining valid insights from their own subconscious minds. And spiritual ideals can certainly help direct one's intent in a direction which will insure that the future becomes a positive experience of "growth" rather than one of "loss" for the soul. The readings also repeatedly state that the closer a soul is in attunement to the Creative Forces, the more apt the soul is to receive insights from the records themselves.

As an example of gaining an insight into the future, Edgar Cayce's secretary, Gladys Davis, had an unusual dream experience which seemed to accurately predict the future of a friend about whom she was concerned. The friend, a Mr. Ladd, was on the verge of losing his job and his family's future looked uncertain. Gladys recalled the background of the experience as follows:

In late January of 1934 Edgar Cayce, Hugh Lynn Cayce [Cayce's eldest son], and I were visitors for the weekend at the Ladd home on Long Island. Late Sunday night Mrs. Ladd was telling me about her husband's financial difficulties; his job was insecure, and they were about to lose their home. As I got in bed I remember wishing I could do something to help the Ladd family. It turned awfully cold that night and I was very uncomfortable. Although the little modern cottage was steam heated, I was from the South and it seemed mighty cold to me.

That evening she had a dream which she would recall and discuss the next morning:

> [In the dream, there was] a knock on the door. I said, "Come in." Mr. Ladd stood there with a coal scuttle in his hand, and wearing a lumber jacket. (I had never seen him in anything but a business suit.) He came in and made a fire in a little coal stove which stood in the room, saying, "Now the room will soon be warm so you can get up."
>
> On the train back to New York later that morning I told Mr. Cayce and Hugh Lynn about the dream, when relating what an uncomfortable night I had experienced. We all laughed and attributed the dream to my discomfort. Still, I remember remarking how strange it was that the room should be different from the one I was occupying—which had cute little radiators on two sides of it (too cute and too little).

Gladys thought no more about the dream until April 1935, fifteen months later, when she was on a business trip to New York and found herself in a guest house at the Sun Air Farm in Oak Ridge, N.J. On Sunday morning, April 7, 1935, she was awakened by the sound of knocking at her door. She said, "Come in" and, according to Gladys, "there stood Mr. Ladd in his lumber jacket, a coal bucket in his hand, and he said, 'I thought you'd like to have a little fire in your stove to take the chill off while you get dressed.' I immediately noticed that the little room was exactly the same as I had dreamed it over a year ago." Apparently, Mr. Ladd had become manager of the Sun Air Farm in January 1935.

Later that June, Gladys asked in a reading how such an experience was even possible. She was told:

> The law of cause and effect is immutable, by choice in individual experience. Or choice is the factor that alters or changes the effect produced by that which is the builder for every experience of associations of man, in even material experience. Hence as thought and purpose and aim and desire are set in motion by minds, their EFFECT is as a condition that IS . . . DREAM is but ATTUNING an individual mind to those individual storehouses of experience that has been set in motion. Hence at times there may be the perfect connection, at others there may be the static of interference by inability of coordinating the own thought to the experience or actuality or fact set in motion. Hence those experiences that are visioned are not only as has been given to some, to be interpreters of the unseen, but to others dreams or as dreamer of dreams, to others as prophecy, to others healing, to others exhortation, to this and that and the other; yet all are of the same spirit. Hence this is the manner as may be seen.

> 262-83

The importance of dreams in revealing insights into

the future is repeatedly discussed in the Edgar Cayce material. In fact, from Cayce's perspective nothing of significance ever happens without it first being foreshadowed in a dream. However, one's personal will remains an important factor even in the face of a "foreshadowed" future.

An excellent example can be found in Scripture in the story of Joseph and his ability to interpret the dreams of Pharaoh (Genesis 41). By correctly interpreting the pharaoh's dreams, Joseph predicts Egypt will have seven years of plenty followed by seven years of famine. As a result of the dreams, Pharaoh decides that the country must mobilize and prepare for the shortage of food. In time, all that Joseph foresaw comes to pass. But because of the country's preparation, the famine is not catastrophic to the people of Egypt. Although the years of drought were probably inevitable, because of weather patterns and the flooding of the Nile, the ways in which the people prepared for and responded to that drought became a matter of free will.

Another possible dream insight into a personal future comes from the story of a man who dreamed of his own death. The dream was not negative, but seemed to focus on an experience that occurred after he had died:

I dreamed that I had died and was standing on a cloud with a bunch of other people who were also dead. It wasn't at all alarming and seemed kind of natural. After a short while, I found myself standing next to an easel (still in the clouds) and painting a picture of a beautiful sailboat. When I was nearly completed, an angel happened to walk by and commented on the beauty of my painting. We got to talking about other things and finally the angel looked me right in the eyes and said, "You know, in order to achieve balance in your next life, you need to incarnate as a woman." I remember speaking with the angel about it for a moment or two longer, and then that was the end of the dream.

In addition to the beauty of the dream, what eventually intrigued the man about his experience was what happened years later while undergoing relationship counseling with his spouse. The counselor told him that he was "too masculine" in his opinions, thought processes, and behaviors. He was advised to begin admiring and cultivating those qualities which were regarded as feminine traits: compassion, empathy, and a being who was much more nurturing. Could the man's dream have foretold an evolving personal future being drawn in place by the Akashic Records?

The possibility that unfolding futures developing within the records are accessible by one's subconscious mind is evident in the true story of Morgan Robertson, a struggling nineteenth-century writer. In 1898 Robertson wrote a novel about an enormous ocean liner which he described as follows: "She was the largest craft afloat and the greatest of the works of men." The ship was larger than anything that had ever been built and had all the amenities of "a first-class hotel . . . a floating city":

Two brass bands, two orchestras, and a theatrical company entertained the passengers during the waking hours; a corps of physicians attended to the temporal, and a corps of chaplains to the spiritual, welfare of all on board, while a well-drilled fire company soothed the fears of nervous ones and added to the general entertainment by daily practice with their apparatus.

She was considered "unsinkable—indestructible" and had been fashioned so that "nineteen water-tight compartments could be closed in half a minute . . . [and even] with nine compartments flooded the ship would still float . . . "

In the novel, the ship was filled with thousands of people who met their death one cold April night when the "unsinkable" vessel struck an iceberg. The name of Robertson's fictional novel was *Futility: The Wreck of the Titan*. Fourteen years after the novel's release, on April 12, 1912, a ship called the *Titanic* left Southampton, England, on her maiden voyage to New York and sank after striking an iceberg. Both vessels could carry several thousand people, and neither had sufficient lifeboats for its passengers. Both ships were able to travel at speeds of twenty-four to twenty-five knots. The *Titan* was described as being 800 feet in length with a displacement of 70,000 tons; and the real *Titanic* measured 882.5 feet and displaced 66,000 tons. Did Morgan Robertson's subconscious mind provide him with a potential reality from the records which became the subject of his novel? Had the Akashic Records made note of a probable future which was fast coming into existence because of the activities of a British shipping company, the White Star line? The striking similarities between the two crafts suggest that that is exactly what happened.

Although rare, on approximately a dozen occasions while giving a reading, Edgar Cayce would suddenly provide the individual with insights into her or his next life. Because of the dynamic of collective and individual free will, generally such insights were not possible. However, on a number of occasions, the Akashic Records had apparently drawn together enough specific potentials to make accessing portions of the information somehow feasible. For a fifty-one-year-old man (5149-1), Cayce began the reading by stating the man's place of birth and then proceeded to discuss the fact that it was very close to the location he would be born in his next experience—Cayce then named the city.

In the reading given to a forty-one-year-old physician, in addition to discussing the soul's strengths, innate urges, and past lives, Cayce commended the woman for her quest for knowledge which she had undertaken primarily "for the greater ability in helping, aiding others." The reading discussed the fact that her soul would likely experience a great development in the present which would enable her "in the next experience [to] bring for the entity a period of manifestation when few will surpass the entity either in the mental, the material or the spiritual life that will be experienced" (872-1).

In 1934, a sixty-eight-year-old Ph.D. and housewife was told that each soul incarnated in each experience as an opportunity for achieving a more consistent alignment with the Creative Forces. To be sure, sometimes a soul went backward in its development because of losses in a particular experience, but the goal was ever advancement. She was told to keep in mind that anything done for the aggrandizement of self would "come to naught" and that anything done for the glorification of the Creator would "come to fruition." The long-term goal was "that the soul, for its own development, may become one with the universal forces or Creative Energies, or God" (708-1).

Because of Cayce's frequent emphasis on the Creator, the Creative Forces, or God, it may be instructive to point out that the readings never focused on the importance of one's religion. From the readings' perspective, any religion which taught the parenthood of the Creator and the brother/sisterhood of all humanity could be helpful in soul growth. In Cayce's cosmology no one is automatically destined for "heaven," and no one is ever relegated to "hell." Ultimately, all souls will receive the same reward: an awareness of their individuality and their oneness with God.

Because of the dynamics of reincarnation, in all likelihood we have all been Christian, we have all been Muslim, we have all been Jewish, we have all been Hindu, Buddhist, atheist, and agnostic. As a means of discovering our connectedness with one another, the readings recommend a comparative study which will lead to the realization that there is but one God and we are each His children:

> . . . COORDINATE the teachings, the philosophies of the east and the west, the oriental and the occidental, the new truths and the old . . . Correlate not the differences, but where all religions meet— THERE IS ONE GOD! "Know, O Israel, the Lord thy God is ONE!"
>
> 991-1

For Cayce, the importance of life was not a matter of one's religion; rather, it was a matter of whether or not an individual could grow in his or her awareness of the *living spirit.* Heaven was not so much a place as it was a state of being which all souls would eventually manifest. As one individual was told, "For you grow to heaven, you don't go to heaven. It is within thine own consciousness that ye grow there" (3409-1).

Throughout the Depression and World War II, Edgar Cayce gave a number of readings which dealt with international relations and activities occurring within various countries and the response individuals might make in their own lives in the face of great hardship and a world at war. Most of these "World Affairs" readings focused on the events of the day, but some gave precognitive insights into humanity's collective future.

Cayce foresaw a promising Aquarian Age which he described as "the Age of the Lily." The readings depict this collective future as an age of purity when individuals, at long last, will come to understand their true relationship to the Creator. It will be a time in the history of the world when each individual realizes her or his responsibility toward all others. Regardless of the standing of any particular nation, there will "be the greater consideration of each individual, each soul being his brother's keeper" (3976-18). That consideration will lead to what Cayce called a "leveling" in which humanity will understand that *all* are equal, and that "each man will live for his fellow man!" (3976-29)

The difference between the future that Cayce could see unfolding in the Akashic Records and the present condition of the world had to do with humanity's search for power rather than the soul's desire to evolve. In our sojourn through space and time we apparently have forgotten our spiritual essence, we have forgotten our true relationship with God:

> Man's answer to everything has been POWER—Power of money, Power of position, Power of wealth, Power of this, that or the other. This has NEVER been GOD'S way, will never be God's way. Rather little by little, line upon line, here a little, there a little, each thinking rather of the other . . .
>
> 3976-8

As to how to bring about this inevitable transformation? In 1939 Cayce provided the prescription:

> Then, there needs be that not so much be set as

to this ritual, or this form, or the other, for any given peoples or any nation, but rather that the individuals in each nation, EVERYWHERE, are to turn again TO the God of the fathers and not in self-indulgence, self-aggrandizement, but more and more of self-effacement.

For as the people of each nation pray, AND then live that prayer, so must the Spirit work.

Then—each of you here—GIVE GOD A CHANCE to show what great blessings He will give to those who love Him. This does not mean that ye, or ANYONE, would condone persecutions anywhere or in any form. For, know ye, His laws fail not—"As ye sow, so shall ye reap."

Man can only begin, then, within himself.

3976-23

Inevitably when an individual looks at the world situation, it is all too easy to feel helpless in regard to whether or not he or she can have the smallest effect upon the future of the planet. In the face of such insurmountable difficulties, what can one person possibly do? And yet, the Cayce readings make it extremely clear that *wherever* individuals find themselves, they have a work to be done. It is a work which is defined by their previous experiences and skills. It is a work which is no more (and no less) important than any other work. And finally, it is a work that the Creator wishes to have accomplished in an effort to bring about the eventual transformation of every single soul in the earth. As Cayce told one man:

. . . in whatever place or position an individual may be—whether in a place of authority, a place of confidence, a place of security or of whatever na-

ture the activity may be—no individual is in such a
position but that he has merited same for the opportunities of manifesting IN SUCH POSITION the
glory of the Father through his activities with his
fellowmen!

1650-1

In May 1943, a sixty-one-year-old widow was told that,
as far as the records were concerned, she still possessed
a future as a writer and would find a channel for her ca-
pabilities in Washington, D.C. Initially, she could find
work as "a critic, as a reviewer." She was encouraged to
move forward with the talent she felt innately. She was
told she would eventually be able to share with others
the spiritual truths she had found within herself. There
was still much that her life could be about.

In looking for further guidance, the woman asked,
"How can I discipline myself at my age to do what is
mine to do?" Cayce responded, "Repeat three times every day, and then listen: 'LORD, WHAT WOULD THOU
HAVE ME DO TODAY?' Have this not as rote. Mean it!"
During the course of her reading, she was also reminded
that each soul had a particular mission to perform, and
she was encouraged to ask herself whether or not she
was working on that mission full time or just now and
then. Regardless of her age, life was a continuous experience. The reading told her:

As has been experienced in the mental self, there
is as much reason to dwell upon the thought from
whence the soul came, as it is upon whence the soul
goeth. For, if the soul is eternal, it always has
been—if it is always to be. And that is the basis, or
the thought of Creative Force, or God. He ever was,
He ever will be. And individuals, as His children, are

a part of that consciousness . . .

Thus the purpose of manifestation in the material plane; that we may apply here a little, there a little, line upon line, precept upon precept, that we may become like Him.

3003-1

The suggestion that the soul's destiny is to become like its Creator is not at all surprising if we are, in fact, His children. The purpose of a lifetime of experiences is primarily to lead individuals to the growing awareness that without their spiritual essence, they would cease to exist. The physical world is essentially a classroom that enables the soul to experience the dynamics of freedom of choice in relationship to cause and effect. From Cayce's perspective, we are not physical bodies with souls, but are souls who happen to be having a learning experience in the earth. The success of our collective education is inevitable. The Akashic Records have so integrally connected themselves with our lives that ultimately we cannot fail. However, the readings believe that this growth in our awareness will only be possible as we reach out to one another and allow the Creator to work through us. The focus is always upon others. The focus is never upon self.

Then, as there has been and is the passage of a soul through time and space, through this and that experience, it has been and is for the purpose of giving more and more opportunities to express that which justifies man in his relationships one with another; in mercy, love, patience, long-suffering, brotherly love.

938-1

Life is an ongoing adventure of purposeful experiences and relationships, enabling individuals to find their true selves. Deep within each soul there is an impelling force guiding that individual to discover *who am I?* In essence, we are all seekers, seeking our true identity and our relationship to the Whole. All too often, we have sought meaning to our lives through all manner of escape, acquisition, addiction, and confusion. And yet, the time will come in the history of the world when individuals everywhere finally realize that—throughout our sojourns through space and time—we have simply been seeking our connection to spirit, our connection to the Creative Forces, our connection to God.

What does the future have in store for us? Each of our futures contains those very relationships we have found challenging, the unfinished business we have continued to put off until tomorrow, and the same difficulties we have repeatedly overlooked or refused to deal with. At the same time, our future will include the almost unfathomable realization of our deep connection to God. Even now, the Akashic Records are continually molding and shaping our enfolding tomorrows so that these things come to pass. With complete objectivity and flawless precision, the universe's supercomputer system is in the process of downloading those very circumstances and events which will perfectly enable all individuals to arrive at their destiny. It's simply a matter of our free will how long it will take us to get there.

Personal Future Reverie

Note: A reverie is best done with another person (reading the reverie like a script), or with oneself first narrating the reverie on a tape and then playing it back in order to experience the exercise. Although any future time period might be chosen, this reverie will let your imagination examine your life seven years from now. Reveries are generally narrated at about one-third the normal rate of speech.

NARRATION:

Get comfortable in your chair (or on a couch) and close your eyes. Take a deep breath, and relax . . . Take another deep breath—breathing in relaxation and calm. Exhale slowly and completely . . . Breathe in deep once again and tell yourself to relax. Continue breathing slowly and completely, all the while listening to the sound of my voice . . . This is an experience you want . . . You are completely safe . . . The whole time you will be in complete control . . . Breathe deeply and relax . . .

Now, I want you to imagine a scene seven years in the future. This is a scene of your life that you've helped to create. For seven years now, you've focused on discovering your true mission in life . . . You've worked on improving and deepening your relationships with all the individuals around you . . . You've worked on discovering a closer relationship to the Creator . . . In seven years, your life has undergone some profound and positive changes—and now you're going to see the results. You are going to see only those things which are positive and helpful . . .

Imagine it is seven years from now. It is Monday morning 10:00 a.m. You are seeing the picture of a life you've helped to create . . . Where are you . . . ? What are you doing . . . ? Who are you with . . . ? Take it all in . . . [pause for 10 seconds]

It's Monday morning, how do you spend the course of each weekday . . . ? Even in the midst of your busy life, how do you stay in touch with your spiritual connection . . . ?

It's a Monday, seven years from now . . . This is the future that you long wished for. This is the tomorrow that you helped to create. How do you feel about this place and your life . . . ? [pause] What is your underlying attitude about your life and the people in it? At home . . . ? At work . . . ? In your community . . . ? [pause] What happened to change that challenging relationship you had seven years ago . . . ? What mental pursuits have you become involved with . . . ? Learning, reading, absorbing into your inner being . . . ? What kinds of books, TV, movies, computer games, or cyberspace adventures do you enjoy being a part of? Look at everything you can see . . . [pause for 10 seconds]

In your imagination, it's seven years from now. From that time and place, think about a word, or a series of words, or a phrase that describes what spiritual qualities have become most manifested in your life . . . [pause] How do other people now describe you (such as your family, your spouse, your parents, your children, your neighbors, your co-workers) . . . ?

What makes this new world of the future and your life in it so special . . . ? How is it that you came to discover your mission in life . . . ? How does it feel to be so satisfied by what you are doing . . . ? Are people around you being helped by what you do . . . ?

Are there special people in your life . . . ? Can you see other individuals around you . . . ? Have you found a better way of dealing with things that are challenging, or stressful . . . ? In a word, or a series of words, can you sum up your life seven years in the future and how you feel about it . . . ? [pause for 10 seconds]

If you can, in your imagination see if you can speak with the "you" seven years from now . . . Is there anything you would like to ask yourself . . . ? Are there questions you have about your future, or do you wish to ask your future self for insights into your present life . . . ? Ask whatever you desire, and then listen . . . [pause for 20 seconds]

Now, gather everything that you've seen together . . . And when you've collected these images of what your life will be like in the future, I want you to think back to the present . . . Imagine it is today, the same day you began this experience . . . See yourself in this time and this place, sitting in your room (or on your couch) . . . It's the present, and you're firmly grounded in this present time, in this present place, right now . . .

Take a deep breath, exhale, and when you are fully centered in the present, you can open your eyes.

Please note: You may wish to record your experience somewhere while it is still fresh in your mind.

Conclusion

For more than forty years of his adult life, Edgar Cayce was able to put himself into some kind of trance state and provide individuals with accurate information, called readings, in response to virtually any question. In this state he was able to perceive a source of information which he called the Akashic Records, or "God's Book of Remembrance." As he gave a reading, Cayce described the procedure as one in which he became a portion of the records themselves. It was while being connected to these records that all manner of information became available to him. Also called the Book of Life, this source was the compilation of every thought, word, and deed that had occurred in space and time since the dawn of creation. And it enabled Cayce to just as easily provide answers into the nature of the universe as he could give insights into an individual's mission in life or a long-standing problem.

Rather than being simply a *place*, the readings emphasized that these records were everywhere. From Cayce's perspective, individuals could literally see the "shadows" of the records in how they spoke, how they thought, and how they interacted with all others. Everything from an individual's qualities and imperfections to past lives and present conditions were somehow accessible. These same records were accessible by the subconscious mind, through dreams, through reveries, and through intuitive and esoteric exercises. The records contained an ever-evolving blueprint of the soul's individuality that repeatedly manifested in every aspect of a person's life. Not only do the Akashic Records store, track, and compile everything about every person in the history of the world, but they continually attempt to guide, educate, and transform everyone to eventually become the very best that they can be.

In 1934 Cayce gave a lecture in which he emphasized the reality of the Akashic Records. He told his audience, "Don't ever think that your life isn't being written in the Book of Life! I found it! I have seen it! It is being written; YOU are the writer!" That same year one of the readings discussed the fact that these records are inscribed on some kind of "etheric energy," similar in nature to the energy of thought. Because these records are literally impressed upon energy, Cayce stated that it would eventually be possible to create a machine that could analyze this energy and subsequently "read" what the records contain (443-5). Although the readings suggested that such a machine would eventually be a reality, even now there are ways in which individuals can get in touch with the records of their soul's history.

Those records which deal with one's past are the accumulation of a soul's talents, experiences, inclinations, and desires. The continuity of this information resides at a soul level and must be dealt with by an individual in the present—for it resides in the form of memory, or "karma." It's not that this karma belongs to another person from another period in history; rather this memory belongs to one's self and therefore must eventually be dealt with individually. In the language of the readings, "Thus the records of each entity are a part of the universal consciousness . . . Not that the individuals in the various appearances are different, for—though they bore different names, different characteristics—they are one . . . " (2246-1)

In the present, the Akashic Records contain the sum total of all we have ever been. They attempt to mold and shape levels of human consciousness. They draw individuals to experiences and other people as a means of giving them the opportunity to learn from one another. As far as Cayce was concerned, wherever an individual finds him- or herself in the present, that very situation has the potential to be a purposeful one. Each soul enters each experience for a reason, "For, a birth into materiality is not by chance, but that the will of the Creative Forces may make manifest in the experience" (2073-2). Whether or not an individual decides to use the present as a positive, learning experience remains a matter of free will.

The Akashic Records of the future embody an ever-changing array of possibilities and potentials. They are the shadows of things which may be, totally dependent upon what one does in the present with what he or she has learned from the past. They draw together probable events and situations which will best enable each individual to come to know one's self. Ever-changeable, they are integrally connected to the will and what an individual does with her or his present opportunities: " . . . for the destiny of each soul is in what the entity does about the application of creative influences and forces in its own experience in any environ" (820-1). One's future is dependent not upon what one knows, but on how well one applies what one knows.

Beginning in 1933 Cayce gave a series of twenty-three readings to members of an ecumenical prayer group in which he discussed the connection between the Akashic Records and the Book of Revelation. According to Cayce, the Book of Revelation—which was written by St. John when he was in exile on the isle of Patmos—was actually a first-person account of an individual's experience in awakening consciousness. As John meditated, the "seals" of the Book of Life were somehow opened to him and he began to see evidence of his own heightened awareness. In the same manner that the Akashic Records had to be interpreted, the vision experienced by John was rich with symbolism. From Cayce's perspective, the seven candlesticks, the seven seals, the seven churches, and the seven stars were all connected to seven spiritual centers or "chakras" within the human body. These chakras maintain an awareness of the soul's history through space and time and will be awakened as individuals grow in their awareness that they are fundamentally spiritual beings, children of the one God. This personal awakening and growth in consciousness is destined to occur for every individual in the earth.

> Hence the purposes for each soul's experience in materiality are that the Book of Remembrance may be opened that the soul may know its relationship to its Maker.
>
> 1215-4

Edgar Cayce believed that each of us writes the story of our lives through our thoughts, our deeds, and our interactions with those around us. The accumulation of this data is stored in the universe's computer system, the Akashic Records. These records are a portion of the Creative Forces. They have been the source for dreams and inspiration. They have been the substance of archetypes and myth and are deeply interwoven with patterns of human behavior and experience. Containing a repository of our past experiences, these records constantly influence our present situations and circumstance. The ways in which we continually deal with our lives sets in motion potentials and probabilities which are drawn to us from the same records. For that reason, Edgar Cayce believed that any insights we might gain from the Akashic Records themselves can provide us with information about the nature of who we are and our true relationship to the rest of creation—the very information contained in *The Real Book of Life.*

A.R.E. Press

The A.R.E. Press publishes books, videos, and audiotapes meant to improve the quality of our readers' lives—personally, professionally, and spiritually. We hope our products support your endeavors to realize your career potential, to enhance your relationships, to improve your health, and to encourage you to make the changes necessary to live a loving, joyful, and fulfilling life.

For more information or to receive a free catalog, call:

1-800-723-1112

Or write:

A.R.E. Press
215 67th Street
Virginia Beach, VA 23451-2061